Are You The Lady From The Welfare?

Memoirs of a Local Authority Social Worker

by

Alison Thompson

Pen Press

First published in Great Britain by Pen Press

All paper used in the printing of this book has been made from wood grown in managed, sustainable forests.

ISBN13: 978-1-906710-53-8

Printed and bound in the UK
Pen Press is an imprint of Indepenpress Publishing Limited
25 Eastern Place
Brighton
BN2 1GJ

A catalogue record of this book is available from the British Library

Cover design by Jacqueline Abromeit

To all those beleaguered social workers up and down the land who always try to do their best.

Author Biography

Alison Thompson was born and brought up in Hertfordshire, and has written a memoir about the troubled days of her youth in the 40s and 50s, *But What About Me?*

After reading German and French at Bristol University she undertook a 2 year postgraduate social studies course at Sheffield University, and worked in Sheffield as a newly qualified and very green young social worker in the city for 3 years. These 5 years in the "swinging 60s" were busy and happy ones, and also turned out to be a steep learning curve.

The author then took up residence in another part of Northern England, and eventually resumed her social work career, but this time in a largely rural setting. In 2001 she decided it was definitely time to retire. She is married with one daughter.

Prologue

At the outset of my career social workers were looked up to and respected. In recent years, however, only the downside of local authority social work has been publicised by the media — scandals in children's homes, less than satisfactory work carried out with child abuse cases, for example. Unfortunately the good work done by social workers every day all over Britain is not reported on the front page of the tabloids, nor does it form the headlines of the 10 o'clock news. The social worker has become one of society's scapegoats or punchbags, and the general public have been led to believe that we became the baddies of the second half of the 20th century.

Social workers are notoriously inept at standing up for themselves. Whenever a fresh sensation involving an abused child or pensioner left to starve in a cheerless flat bursts upon the scene, and an accusing finger is pointed at social workers, there is usually a deafening silence from the social work fraternity.

I am standing up on behalf of my beleaguered fellow social workers by writing this book, which aims to show the inside story of social work and all the hurdles we strive to overcome, not to mention some of the extraordinary situations and people we come up against.

Memoirs and reminiscences have been written by doctors, nurses, politicians, nannies, taxi drivers, and antique dealers — to name but a few. Nothing seems to have been written by social workers. Such a book is long overdue.

In the Sixties my clients called me "The Lady From The

Welfare". In more modern times fashionable terminology such as "care manager" means nothing to the elderly. Some have not even arrived at the term"social worker". When I retired I was still, to them, "The Lady From The Welfare."

Part I

Chapter One

'They won't like you, you know. Northerners never like Southerners.' Train doors slammed. The guard raised his arm, whistle to lips.

Leaning slightly out of the window as the train prepared to depart, I stared, dismayed, at my mother standing on the platform as she uttered this sudden pronouncement. Heaven only knows, I felt nervous enough at the prospect of this voyage into the unknown without doom-laden predictions from my mother.

With a jerk and a grunt, the train started to roll slowly and self-importantly along the track away from the waving, running friends and relatives left behind. Soon the vast edifice of St Pancras receded into the murky distance, and the train gradually gathered momentum as it made its ponderous way through the jumbled sprawl of north London.

It was 1964. Skirts were still below the knee. Cilla Black was a slip of a 19-year-old with white lipstick and kohl-rimmed eyes. The E-type Jag had been an obsessive topic of conversation amongst my male student friends at Bristol University, from which I had just graduated. Now I was on my way North to embark on a postgraduate diploma course in social studies, with the aim of becoming a social worker.

A social worker! As I nestled into my seat by the window and watched the never-ending parade of houses, fields, sheep, ribbon-like roads, church spires, gas works, factories flitting

1

past the grubby glass, I thought to myself: but I don't even want to be a social worker.

Bookish and dreamy, I had never so far hankered after any career. In fact, I was well into my third year at Bristol when it began to dawn on me that I would be obliged to make plans and focus my mind on jobs. My father had grandiose ideas about my future. One day during the summer vacation, he had called me into his study and announced that with a modern languages degree I could carve out a career in the Foreign Office. This lofty suggestion having met with a negative response on my part, my father retorted, a note of exasperation creeping into his voice, 'You'll have to earn your living somehow, you know.'

I must have been a sore disappointment to my ambitious parents. When it became crystal clear that I had not, alas, inherited my father's first-class scientific brain, he decided to relinquish the dreams of his younger daughter emerging as a latter-day Pasteur or Faraday, and zoom in on what I did show a flair for – languages and literature. Hence the idea about the Foreign Office.

During my adolescence I was an enthusiastic cinema goer, and loved not only the films but the whole atmosphere of the cinema, including the purchase of a choc ice from the usherette in the interval and the mad rush to consume it before it started melting over one's clothes and onto the floor as the lights dimmed once more. I envied the usherette's good fortune in being able to see all the films every week several times over. In an attempt at appeasement, I suggested brightly to my father that I could perhaps acquire a job as cinema usherette. This idea did not go down well.

The university careers advice people found me equally uninspiring. The formidable lady with the severely plucked eyebrows seated behind an imposing desk eyed me disparagingly and tried to propel me into agreeing to a teacher training course. I hastily declined and added that my mother, who had been a teacher herself, did not consider me to be 'teacher material'. Plucked eyebrows gave me another withering look. 'At your age you should have grown out of being influenced by your mother,' she declared in a clipped voice and shut the file in front of her with a brisk snap. 'If it's not to be teaching, then it will have to be social work.' Thus was my future decided upon.

Outside the train window a church with a crooked spire swam sharply into focus, and the hurrying train slowed slightly as it thundered through a station and on past a blur of buildings. Chesterfield. Another half hour or so and the journey would be over.

Windows were pushed smartly down and handles turned. Doors flew open as the train grumbled slowly to a halt. Clumsily I stumbled onto the platform with my two heavy cases. Where were the taxis? I looked round for a sign. The milling crowd, hurrying or strolling in all directions, jostled me as I stood perplexed, the flat Northern vowels sounding somehow alien and un-British to my South Eastern ears.

'Want any help, luv?' I felt a hand on my shoulder and turned round. There behind me stood a shortish, plump man in a BR uniform, a friendly grin on his round, pink face.

'Oh, yes please – I need to get a taxi.' Without more ado the rotund official seized my cases, said 'Follow me, luv', and walked briskly towards the taxi rank, where he handed me and my luggage over to an equally friendly driver of a black cab.

How different from the London taxi drivers, I reflected, who appeared to regard their fares as irritating nuisances with, nonetheless, bottomless purses, and who would never so much as deign to budge from their seats to help people struggling with luggage.

The driver clambered into his seat and twisted round towards me. 'Where to, lass?'

'Glossop Road, please, number 425.' I perched tensely on the edge of the seat and peered out into the hazy September afternoon as the black taxi drew slowly away from the forecourt of the Midland Station, and manoeuvred its way into the dense, crawling traffic. I had arrived.

Thus began a five-year love affair with the big, brash city of Sheffield.

Chapter Two

Then, as now, practical 'placements' played a key role in social work training. My very first placement was with the Sheffield probation service, and I was plunged straight into this two days after my arrival.

Anne Tryon was my supervisor. Mannish, even slightly butch, Miss Tryon was habitually attired in plain dark suits and sensible brogues. Sartorially, she reminded me of my divinity teacher at school, Miss Dunbar, she of the pudding basin haircut who had never worn anything other than grey suits and the Dunbar tartan tie. There, however, the resemblance ended. Miss Tryon, probably in her 50s, was of upper middle class stock and as a girl had attended Cheltenham Ladies College. I pondered as to why such a person should have chosen to become a probation officer.

This month spent with the probation service, my initial foray into a completely new world, consisted largely of accompanying Miss Tryon on home visits to clients and their families and of going to the magistrates' court to observe the procedures. After two weeks I started attending court sessions several times a week on my own, clutching a notebook and pencil with the aim of describing in writing the course of each case. Early on, however, I came across a big obstacle – language. The Sheffield accent and dialect were a total mystery to me. Never having lived further North than Bristol, I felt I had arrived in a foreign land, although geographically speaking, Sheffield is in the dead centre of England. Sheffielders, however, regard themselves as very much Northerners and part of Yorkshire.

Much of what I scribbled down turned into fiction. Since at least 50 per cent of what was said in court was incomprehensible to me, in desperation I invented most of the facts of each case. The only people I could understand were the solicitors, magistrate and probation officers, and even some of these spoke fairly broad Yorkshire. Somewhat surprisingly, Miss Tryon never questioned the validity of my notes.

It soon became clear to me that Miss Tryon's appearance and superior demeanour were no bar to a genuine rapport between her and her clientele. Seated on a shabby bed in a sparsely furnished flat conversing with an offending 19-year-old, or behind her desk at the office listening sympathetically while the stout wife of a man on probation for persistent pub brawls expounded her particular way of dealing with her husband's misdemeanours ('If he come home sober, Miss, he gets a nice plate of egg and chips, but if he come back full o'drink he gets nowt but a plain buttie'), she was completely at ease, despite the gulf between her own social background and that of her clients.

Occasionally I was permitted to visit clients or their families on my own, usually to convey some kind of straightforward message from Miss Tryon, not to become involved in an interview. Here, too, lingo was an issue, and not only in people's homes. One afternoon I became hopelessly lost in Attercliffe, a downtown area of the city, while trying to find the address of a recalcitrant teenage boy. I was to hand over a letter from Miss Tryon to his mother. A woman in fluffy bedroom slippers with her hair done up in rollers (I had already observed with astonishment that a large number of Sheffield women went around all day shopping, travelling on buses and so on with roller-covered heads) was leaning nonchalantly against a wall between two houses.

'Excuse me,' I enquired hesitantly, 'could you tell me where Francis Street is?' I carefully pronounced 'Francis' with a flat Yorkshire 'a' as I had observed Miss Tryon doing when speaking to the indigenous population. The woman pointed across the road. 'Go up ginnel, luv, turn right, and that'll bring you into Francis Street.'

What was this 'ginnel' that I had to go up? Perhaps it was some kind of hill or slope, or could it be a flight of steps? The woman obviously sensed my confusion. 'Come on, luv, I'll cross road wi' you.' Shuffling in her fluffy slippers, she led the way to the opposite pavement and stopped at the entrance to a narrow alleyway between two rows of terraced houses. 'Here's ginnel, lass. Go straight along.' Thus my linguistic education slowly progressed.

At the end of each day of this initiation into a hitherto unknown area of life, I returned home totally exhausted with the effort of absorbing new experiences and chunks of knowledge. Home was an attic room above a suite of offices, chosen for me by Edna and Liza Marsh, two spinster sisters and friends of my mother and grandmother who had been living in Sheffield for many years. This attic bedsit was on the university's 'approved' accommodation list. In 1964 male and female students were still not permitted to share accommodation, and on either side of me were other bedsits also rented by female students. I shared the kitchen and bathroom with the office staff who worked below.

From this building could be observed the whole of life. Next door lived a chaotic and rumbustious family who were clients, I discovered, of the Family Service Unit. There were seven children in total, most of whom had different fathers, either totally absent or putting in an appearance on an occasional basis. All the children, aged between 18 months and 12 years, went barefoot in all weathers and seasons, including snow. The mother, a surprisingly tiny woman with short, spiky hair, appeared to spend most of her time seated on a battered kitchen chair on the threshold of the ever-open street door, watching the comings and goings of the neighbourhood and now and again rebuking one or other of her unruly brood.

From my attic window I could see the exclusive little private school on the other side of the road, once a substantial Victorian private house, and watch the well-dressed mothers or au pair girls arrive in smart cars and deposit young children, clad in pristine uniform, at the school gate. Through the open window the sounds of polished, upper middle class accents wafted upwards, contrasting oddly with the broad Sheffield voices of passers-by. The inequalities of British society were beginning to become evident to me.

Glossop Road was already, in the Sixties, a busy thorough-fare. From the kitchen on the first floor I looked across to a small unclaimed area of countryside, consisting of thick undergrowth and a number of mature trees. During the daytime the only sound to be heard was the roar and rumble of traffic, travelling towards Derbyshire in one direction and the city centre in the other. At quieter times, for instance very early in the morning, melodious birdsong arose from these trees and bushes. During my first spring in Sheffield I heard the cuckoo announce his triumphant presence several times – and this only half a mile from the busiest part of the town.

This little bucolic oasis in the midst of urban sprawl soon disappeared, however. A year or two after my arrival in Glossop Road, gangs of workmen complete with earthmovers, bulldozers and other monstrous machines decimated the trees and scrub, and churned up the earth. Bricks and mortar, glass and steel rose ever higher and became a building, then a complex of buildings. Like a Phoenix the Royal Hallamshire Hospital, eventually to become one of Britain's foremost teaching hospitals, had arisen from the wasteland. The call of the cuckoo was a sound of the past.

About 500 yards further up the road, nearer the shops in the area known as Broomhill, one came to a narrow lane which ran at right angles to Glossop Road. Down this 'ginnel', some 20 years later, the police finally caught up with and arrested the serial killer known as the Yorkshire Ripper.

—oOo—

My month's placement with the probation service was soon over, and it was time to begin my academic course at the university. At the beginning of October I joined my fellow postgraduate students for the first lectures and seminars of the term.

The senior lecturer in charge of the diploma course was Eric Sainsbury, later to become Professor of Social Administration. Mr Sainsbury was a Christian. A true Christian is a rarity. Unlike many who call themselves Christians, Eric Sainsbury did not live within a bigoted straitjacket, and was no whited sepulchre. He kept modestly quiet about his faith, and in fact I had been at the university for several months before I discovered that he and his wife were practising Anglicans and, moreover, had quietly taken into their home one of my fellow students and his pregnant girlfriend, both of whom were penniless. I was then, and am now, a godless woman, yet have respect for those of whatever religion who actually follow the tenets laid down by their particular gods.

There was about Mr Sainsbury a slightly precious air enhanced by his predilection for velvet jackets. He endeared himself to us by his tendency towards self-deprecation and entertained us with anecdotes from his earlier days. After reading English at Balliol he had come to the conclusion that the gaining of an English degree was not one iota of use to anyone except himself, and wondered what to do with his life. 'I know what I'll do,' he thought to himself, 'I'll become a probation officer.' So he did. After some years in the probation service he then entered the world of university teaching.

As a child he had been an evacuee, and he enjoyed recounting to his students the story of how he had been one of a group of children all with labels bearing their names round their necks. On arriving at their destination in the country, each child was collected by the person or family on whom he or she was to be billeted. One by one the children were eyed and weighed up by these adult strangers, each of whom was clearly intent on choosing the most attractive or least scruffy child on offer. All were eventually chosen – all, that is, except Eric, who was left standing all alone with his label round his neck, feeling like an abandoned suitcase. Such anecdotes were always linked to some topic we were studying – for instance, the history of research into child development. The profoundly disturbing effect that evacuation had on thousands of children during the war years provided a valuable insight into how children react to loss and change, particularly when placed with foster parents or in children's homes.

The Social Studies syllabus, along with the practical placements, opened up a whole new and sometimes bewildering world to me, coming as I did straight from years of immersion in a linguistic and literary sphere.

Social administration, psychology, social history, anthropology, sociology, philosophy, social medicine, and the study of chosen specialist subjects such as the history of mental ill-health in Britain and its treatment – all this, in the form of lectures, discussion groups, and essay and thesis writing, now filled my days.

We joined first year medical students for psychiatry lectures. Professor Stengel, well known for his books on suicide, presided over these, entering the large lecture hall with a theatrical flourish, clearly relishing this opportunity to play to the gallery. Always an avid people watcher, I tended to sit towards the back of the hall, quite high up amongst the tiers of benches, in order to observe the assembled company. The undergraduate medics, most of them still in their teens, seemed alarmingly juvenile. Was the health of the nation to be in the hands of these adolescent boys and girls, I wondered, feeling infinitely more mature at the superior age of 22. One hoped that at the end of their five years basic training these aspiring doctors would have progressed some way along the path towards greater maturity.

In addition to the standard text books on casework theory etc – some of which, for example Florence Hollis's lengthy tome, were almost unbearably tedious – we were also supplied with a general book list of fiction and non-fiction works, all depicting in some way the social history of Britain, and we were encouraged to read as many books on this list as possible. A passionate reader since the age of four, I needed little encouragement. Thus I was introduced to new literary experiences, including the delectable *Lark Rise to Candleford* by Flora Thompson. Eric Sainsbury was a great fan of the novels of Angus Wilson, also on the book list, and was apt to remark that social work students needed no training other than the perusal of Wilson's books.

My fellow students were a motley assortment. I quickly observed that many of them were older than I; in fact, their ages ranged from 21 to something over 50. At once I felt I fitted in with this group. At Bristol I had never felt at ease with my peers, and had begun to wonder if I were the only young person around who was less than enthusiastic about parties and pop music. Moreover, Bristol University was in my undergraduate days, and possibly still is, an establishment of quite outstanding snobbishness. To give an example of this, it should perhaps be mentioned that I and two friends (all three of us had been pupils at traditional girls' grammar schools) applied for places in one of the halls of residence at the beginning of our second year. The warden of this particular hall, an autocratic harridan, turned us down on the grounds that we did not emanate from public school backgrounds, which a high percentage of students at Bristol came from. No girls from state schools – was this policy really very different from stating 'No Jews' or 'No blacks'?

This group of postgraduate students at Sheffield, however, came from all walks of life and were refreshingly unbiased and unbuttoned up. The older students had all pursued other careers before deciding to change course and embark on social work training. The younger ones amongst us were mainly fresh from degree courses, green, and with little experience of either life or the world of work.

The aforementioned young man who lodged with the Sainsburys, together with his girlfriend, had been a fellow student of mine at Bristol, and likewise read German. It was pure coincidence that we decided on the same postgraduate course in the same city. I came to know him better in Sheffield than I ever had in Bristol. Half Yugoslavian on his father's side, he was fond of recounting how his mother, as a young Englishwoman with a yen for travel, had taken up a post as governess in the Yugoslav royal family at King Peter's court, and eventually married a native of the country.

Another of our group, a young man called Geoff Pearson, liked to make it known that he had been a contemporary of David Frost at Cambridge. Eric Sainsbury once remarked in my hearing that 'young Pearson will go far, mark my words'. One day, many years later, I was listening to the Jimmy Young show while loading the washing machine. The topic under discussion was juvenile delinquency, and in particular criminal tendencies amongst young boys. Invited on to the show that morning to give his views was 'the expert on criminology, Professor Geoffrey Pearson'. My mind having been brusquely diverted from the task in hand, I found myself trying to load the radio into the machine and put the cat's dinner under the grill! Yes, young Pearson had indeed gone far!

In our spare time we tended to congregate in the university refectory and put the world to rights with endless lively discussions and arguments. Harold Wilson's victory in the autumn of 1964 was an exciting highlight for all of us, with most of us glued to our radios all night after election day (few of us possessed TVs) as the results came in.

Even the irreligious amongst us were gripped by the wind of change blown through the Church by the Bishop of Southwark and the movement dubbed 'the New Reformation'. Politics and religion, difficult landlords or the pros and cons of the new fangled tights that were appearing on the hosiery scene – all were equally absorbing topics of conversation.

During this first year of training we had to undertake two more practical placements, one with the Sheffield Council for Voluntary Service and the other at the Royal Infirmary, now largely demolished. These afforded an opportunity not only to open a window onto various areas of social work, but also to mix with postgraduate students from other courses. At the Sheffield Council for Voluntary Service clients I became acquainted with were mainly elderly, whereas within the portals of the Infirmary I came into contact with all age groups. Because this year of training amounted to no more than a basic initiation, I did not take on anything resembling a caseload, but was more of an observer of the social work scene.

My acquaintance with various districts of Sheffield deepened, including the two monstrous blocks of flats near the Midland Station known as Hyde Park and Park Hill. Constructed in the 1950s and declared, with an air of great panache, to be architectural masterpieces, and described in glowing terms by Roy Hattersley in his autobiographical account of his childhood and youth spent in Sheffield, they were in fact, to those who lived in them and those who visited, little short of concrete prisons. Architects do not live in the blocks of flats they design; they merely collect awards and bask in adulation.

One elderly woman I visited lived on the fifth floor. Because the lifts were almost perpetually out of order and rarely put right, and because she was too frail to walk up and down five flights of stairs, she was effectively a prisoner in her own home. Young mothers with grizzling toddlers yanked and bumped prams and pushchairs up and down endless stairways. I likewise climbed many steps. Even when the lifts were working, they were far from salubrious, stinking with urine and full of litter; I avoided using them. Once closeted in one of those malodorous lifts, you never knew what dubious character might become your lift-mate. Le Corbusier had a lot to answer for, I reflected grimly.

At the Royal Infirmary I was attached to one of the hospital social workers, still known then as almoners. I sat in on many an interview while anxious patients or distraught relatives unburdened themselves. Some of the locals had a problem with the word 'almoner'. One morning I was in the office alone when a very small man, clearly a patient as he was clad in a pair of somewhat startling orange and white striped pyjamas (no dressing gown), came tiptoeing in. With a deferential air he murmured, 'Excuse me, miss, is this the Lady Almoaner's department?'

The year passed very quickly. Going out into the world of work and supporting myself could be put off no longer. I was only half trained and knew that at some stage I would undertake the second year of training, the applied social studies course, on which the placements assumed a greater importance, and students took on real, albeit small, caseloads. But for now the need to be financially independent was pressing. My father had died suddenly shortly after Christmas, my mother was struggling to adjust to unexpected widowhood. A full-time job for me was imperative.

Chapter Three

Cats. There were cats everywhere: six on the sofa, seven on the back of the sofa, two black kittens perched on the mantelpiece amongst ornaments and bric à brac. Four more on the floor busily eating scraps off chipped enamel plates. Five assorted kittens clamped to threadbare curtains, apparently perfecting their abseiling skills. Several other furry bodies reclined or romped around my feet.

'Thirty cats you have altogether?' enquired Chris politely. The man standing by the newspaper-covered wooden table, clad in an ill-fitting pair of black trousers clinched at the waist with a piece of string, nodded his head slowly.

'Aye, that's right, lad. And t'landlord says we've got to get out next week, us and the cats, that is.'

This was the second day of my new job with the Social Care Department, a local authority organisation which endeavoured to meet the needs of the elderly and the homeless. I was spending that first week shadowing one of my more experienced colleagues as he visited his clients in various different parts of the city. We had come to call on the Dawsons, a middle-aged couple living in one room with 30 cats whose landlord was not merely threatening eviction, but was about to effect it.

Thirty cats in one room. This was a little overwhelming even for me, the archetypal cat lover. At least the cats looked healthy and not unkempt, in sharp contrast to the Dawsons and their surroundings. There was a distinctive smell in that shabby, dirty room, a smell which had nothing to do with the cats who apparently went outside into the maze of back yards and allotments to do their business. It was an odour with which I was to become only too familiar over the succeeding years, and which lurked in houses that were never cleaned.

Mrs Dawson was tiny and shaped like a cottage loaf, her generous top half balanced on her even more rotund bottom half. She waddled in now through the back door leading to the yard. 'Thank goodness you've come, Mr Perry. What are we going to do?' She stood just inside the door, peering anxiously up at Chris, who had positioned himself by the empty fireplace. Before we entered the house he had warned me against sitting down even if proffered a seat.

'Well,' replied Chris, passing the flat of his hand over his forehead, 'I think I may have found another place for you, but you can't take all the cats. Two or three, perhaps.' Later, as the weeks went by, it became clear to me that Chris knew virtually all the private landlords in Sheffield and was a dab hand at persuading some of them to take on seemingly impossible tenants.

Husband and wife looked at each other in consternation. 'Only two or three?' said Mr Dawson, picking one of the kittens off the mantelpiece and tenderly placing it on the floor by the dishes. 'What will happen to all the rest? I can't bear to think of them becoming strays again.'

'No, that won't happen,' Chris assured him. 'I've had a word with the RSPCA and, if you're agreeable to the idea, one of their inspectors will come and take the cats away and look after them until new homes are found.'

After more discussion and reassurances on Chris's part, we at last stepped outside into the street. I gulped in mouthfuls of fresh air. As with my first placement with the probation service, I was being plunged straight into the realities of social work. It remained to be seen whether I would sink or swim.

In the Sixties almost full employment was the order of the day. Unemployment and redundancy were not words which peppered everyone's daily conversation. I and another girl from the social studies course had found jobs with the social care department with ease, following interviews and medicals. This was an era of expansion in social work, and the various social work departments (the concept of all client groups being dealt with under the unifying umbrella of the Social Services Department had yet to be born) were keen to take on qualified social workers. The latter were a relatively new animal, and their introduction into social work departments created a feeling of tension between them and the old established, largely unqualified welfare officers, many of them recruited from the forces in the immediate post-war years.

Our salary was £820 per annum, which to me seemed an awesome sum. With my very first month's pay at the end of October 1965, I bought, feeling like a daring spendthrift, a Royal Worcester coffee pot and three matching cups and saucers. They are still counted amongst my most prized possessions.

That introductory week during which I shadowed Chris was soon over, and thereafter I took on my own caseload. I was essentially on my own, visiting clients and interviewing them on a one-to-one basis. No more trying to merge quietly with the wallpaper while the 'real' social worker dealt with the client. Although supervised in the office by an older member of staff, I was now essentially that real social worker out in the field.

In addition to Chris Perry, who years later climbed to the top to become Director of South Glamorgan Social Services Department, two other of my fellow colleagues were also embryonic high flyers, but at that stage still very junior basic rate social workers. Blond, charming, with a slight swagger to his walk, Mike Bishop was the office beau with an eye for a skirt. Skirts were rising at a rate of knots now, and we young women (and one or two older ones) vied with each other to see how far up our thighs we dared let our skirts or dresses ride. Ironically, it was still against departmental rules for women to wear trousers, but no one uttered a word of disapproval about our microscopic mini skirts. Possibly this was because all the senior managers were male.

Like Chris, Mike Bishop also rose to the top of the social services tree, and eventually became Director of Cleveland Social Services. Towards the end of the Eighties the child abuse scandal burst upon the scene and became front page news, with the names of Dr Marietta Higgs and Michael Bishop on everyone's lips in living rooms, pubs, and places of work. Looking at the familiar face, scarcely touched by the passing of the years, appearing on the TV screen or gazing up at me from pictures in newspapers and social work journals, I thought back to those youthful days in the Social Care Department and pictured in my mind's eye Mike sitting at his desk by the window in our open plan office, flirtatious, extrovert and already, at the age of 24, sparking with ambition.

Chris, Mike, I and Martin Manby were all exactly the same age, and we all had birthdays within a few months of each other. Some wag in the office decided to nickname us the quadruplets, and this appellation stuck.

Martin was a singularly nice young man. Shortly before my arrival in the department he had married, and I soon became quite friendly with him and his wife, Christine. She took me out for driving practice in her battered Mini, and we indulged in many a laugh – and several hair-raising moments – as I toiled up and down the series of hills on which Sheffield is built. My formal driving lessons with a bullying and intimidating driving instructor whose personality certainly contained a steak of sadism had proved to be disastrously unsuccessful. In no uncertain terms he had declared that I was incapable of learning to drive. Practising with Christine was a relaxing contrast.

My lessons with the instructor took place outside Sheffield, as he lived in North Derbyshire. The loveliness of the Peak District was lost on me as I strove vainly and timorously to master the basic skills of driving. During one such painful instruction period, we were driving along a narrow minor road which seemed, rather puzzlingly, to be dwindling into a rutted track. Suddenly a gesticulating figure materialised some yards ahead of us on the track, and I noted with a shock that he was brandishing some sort of firearm. Judging by his body language, he was consumed with fury.

'Oh Christ!' muttered my instructor, 'it's one of the local farmers. We'll have to get out of this lane as fast as we can.'

It was 1967, and foot and mouth disease had struck the farming community. I was aware of this fact but, in common probably with most city dwellers had, I confess, given it little thought. Now it dawned on me that we should have avoided what was probably a farm track.

How was I to get back to the main road? Should I reverse all the way, or should I attempt a three-point turn in this very narrow boggy lane?

I decided to reverse and put my foot down hard. I had not conveyed my intentions to the instructor, and, to my utter consternation the car, instead of retreating swiftly, shot forward, almost running over the toes of the advancing farmer. I had pressed my foot on the accelerator!

'You bloody little fool!' yelled my mentor. 'Reverse, reverse!'

In moments of extreme fear or stress my mind goes totally blank. This was one such moment of temporary dementia and I forgot completely how to set about reversing a car. Fortunately this car had dual controls and the instructor adroitly took over, the car backing steadily towards the A road we had recently left.

Once there, we took off quite smartly, anxious to put as much road space as possible between us and the enraged farmer, whom I could see in the mirror at the entrance to the lane, wildly waving his gun, much to the consternation of other motorists.

It was at that point that my instructor, with biting sarcasm, informed me that I would never make a driver.

Tearfully and fearfully I travelled back by train to the centre of Sheffield, walked into a large department store and purchased a small teddy bear as I felt in need of comfort. Impulse buying was not something in which I often indulged, but the sight of this forlorn teddy, the only one among a whole pile of neatly wrapped and beribboned teddies on the counter without a cellophane wrapping or ribbon, struck a chord. I have always felt sorry for runts and outcasts.

An ability to drive is an obvious advantage for a social worker, but for now I would stick to the buses. There was, after all, at that time a cheap and excellent bus service in Sheffield. I wished to have no more to do with either sadistic driving instructors or homicidal farmers. To this day I can see in my mind's eye the farmer's purple face, distorted with fury, and I am convinced that he would have killed us if he had managed to reach us. If I was the cause of spreading the foot and mouth virus further around Derbyshire through my panic and incompetence, it was very definitely done unwittingly.

In the fullness of time Martin also became a Director, first of the London Borough of Greenwich, and then of Sheffield. He has also appeared on TV, on one occasion on the 9 o'clock news. Like Chris and Mike, he had journeyed a long way from those lowly, impecunious days in Sheffield. On one occasion Martin and Christine dished me up a lunch of bangers and mash, followed by apple meringue, in their rented flat. They could only afford the cheapest food, but were unperturbed by this hard-up state of affairs.

In common with my colleagues, my caseload consisted of a mixture of 'elderly' cases and cases of families who were either on the brink of homelessness or had actually become homeless.

In the Sixties extreme longevity was not quite so commonplace as it is now, but there were still a considerable number of elderly who became physically or mentally frail – or both – and who needed help from various agencies. One of the most bizarre cases concerning an elderly person I have ever had to deal with was that of a retired dentist in his 70s. Still living in the flat above the surgery, he was afflicted with quite severe dementia and firmly believed that he was still a full-time practising dentist. In fact, he had retired 13 years previously.

This elderly man not only believed he was still a dentist, but was actually operating as one, opening up the surgery every day and receiving patients. Those who in earlier times had been his regular patients did not attend, needless to say, but unsuspecting people, passing through Sheffield or staying in the city for a day or two for a variety of reasons and suddenly needing urgent medical attention, would ring at the door on catching sight of the gleaming brass plate. 'L. Pomfret, Dental Surgeon' was engraved thereon. Neighbours regularly caught sight of him on the doorstep lovingly polishing this plate.

Mr Pomfret's disturbing activities were brought to the Social Care Department's attention by his son, who had been alerted by worried neighbours. I was asked to visit him to see if any kind of intervention would alleviate the situation. With hindsight, it seems reasonable to question whether an inexperienced social worker should have been expected to handle a tricky case such as this.

Feeling not a little apprehensive, I climbed the steps to the solid, bottle green front door of the Victorian terraced house in Eccleshall Road. I paused, my finger already outstretched to push the bell. Not a sound could be heard from within, no voices, no whine of a drill. Perhaps Mr Pomfret had no patients today. I rang the bell firmly and waited.

Shuffling footsteps could be heard on the other side of the door, which now opened a crack. A man poked his head out, a head framed by a magnificent mane of wavy white hair.

'Mr Pomfret?' I enquired brightly. 'I'm from the Social Care Department, and I've come—'

'Do come in,' said the elderly man, cutting me off in mid sentence, and opened the door wider. He stepped back and beckoned to me to follow him along the gloomy, high-ceilinged hall. At an open doorway leading into a large room halfway down the corridor, he paused and invited me to go through. Thinking this must be some kind of living room, I walked in with the intention of sitting down and attempting a tactful chat with Mr Pomfret.

This was no living room, however. I gasped as I caught sight of the dentist's chair by the window with an array of shining instruments set out beside it and, above them, two drills. I swung round and stepped quickly out into the hall, just in time to see Mr Pomfret closing the front door firmly, locking it and slipping the large key into his trouser pocket.

He shuffled back down the hall, took me firmly by the elbow and propelled me back into the surgery. 'Now, if you'll just seat yourself in the chair over there, I'll have a look at your teeth. What trouble are we having, then? Any toothache?'

'But Mr Pomfret, I haven't come to have my teeth seen to, I've just come to have a talk with you. Your son is rather worried about you.'

My voice trailed away as I realised that Mr Pomfret's brain was clearly not registering what I was saying. He simply saw me as a patient who had come to him for dental treatment. What did a social worker do in circumstances such as these? I had no idea.

Like many people, I had a particular fear of dentists – even of ordinary, sane dentists. This was no visit to an ordinary dentist, however, this macabre encounter with a demented pensioner who was convinced that I was in need of his dental expertise.

Despite his 77 years, Mr Pomfret was surprisingly strong, and I found that I was unable to free myself from his grasp as he pushed me determinedly towards the chair. Heart pounding, I half fell, half clambered on to it. Perhaps I could keep him talking and even persuade him to give me the key to the front door.

Mr Pomfret, however, meant business. He jerked my head back and obliged me to open my mouth with a deft flick of his thumb and forefinger, in the manner of a skilful vet prising apart the jaws of a reluctant cat or dog on the examination table. With one hand he kept my mouth open while with the other he selected one of the shining instruments neatly laid out.

At that moment the front door bell rang shrilly. Mr Pomfret paused, his head turned towards the door. 'Oh, that must be the next patient. Please could you wait a moment while I let them in.' Whereupon he relinquished my jaw, trudged off across the surgery and vanished into the hall. Quick as a flash I bounded out of the chair and ran out into the corridor. Just inside the front door stood a young woman in a nurse's uniform. Mr Pomfret had already closed the door behind her and was in the act of turning the key in the lock.

'I'm from the Social Care Department but I can't get Mr Pomfret to understand that I'm not a patient,' I blurted out.

'And I'm Denise Bramall, district nurse,' the girl explained. 'I knew you were coming and I arranged with Mr Pomfret's son to meet you and him here so that we could try and thrash out a plan of action.' She glanced furtively at Mr Pomfret, who was trying to usher us both along the corridor and into the surgery. 'He's got two of us locked in now,' she murmured. 'I wonder how many more prisoners he plans to collect.'

Feeling bolder now that I had an ally or fellow captive, I decided to stand my ground and resist being pushed back to that sinister chair. We told Mr Pomfret politely but firmly that we would wait by the front door until his son arrived.

'My son?' Mr Pomfret raised his bushy white eyebrows and a puzzled look stole over his face. 'I haven't got a son, have I?'

'Of course you've got a son, Dad, and here I am,' suddenly announced a voice from the nether regions, and a man of about 40 appeared through a door at the far end of the hall. 'I parked my car down a side street and let myself in through the back door.'

He bore a striking resemblance to his father, although the fine head of hair was dark and the chiselled features unlined. Looking quizzically at me he asked, 'Are you the lady from the welfare?' Whereupon he laid a kindly hand on his father's shoulder and suggested he went upstairs to his private flat. Mr Pomfret did not move. The puzzled look remained on his face and he suddenly appeared what in actual fact he was – a confused and bewildered old man.

'Come on, we'll go up together and I'll put the kettle on.' Mr Pomfret junior gently pushed his father in the direction of the flight of stairs leading up to the first floor. 'Wait here, you two, and when I've got Dad settled I'll come down again and we'll have a chinwag.'

Two hours later I made my weary way back to the office on the bus. After much discussion it had been decided that Mr Pomfret must be removed from the house. The family GP, assisted by Denise – both liked and trusted by the old man – would be asked to exercise a little tactful persuasion and steer him towards voluntary admission to Middlewood, the local psychiatric hospital.

After that, I would enter the scene again, with the aim of gaining Mr Pomfret's agreement to take up a long-stay place in an elderly persons' home. Whether this would be difficult or relatively problem-free remained to be seen.

Chapter Four

Not all the work consisted of carrying out home visits. There was much written work and telephoning to do, and also something called office duty. We social workers took it in turns to stay in the office and attend to people who arrived on the premises with a query or a problem. Much of this was routine, humdrum stuff, but some of the encounters were difficult and stressful, or even laced with menace.

One of my colleagues, a girl called Linda, had to deal one afternoon with two enormous Irishmen, both in their cups. It transpired that they were brothers, and working with one of the many gangs of construction workers then engaged in the considerable amount of demolition of old houses and erection of huge new blocks of flats taking place in the city. This was an era of preoccupation with the destruction and construction of buildings. The two men wanted to bring their frail elderly mother over from Southern Ireland to live in Sheffield, and, as they themselves were living in temporary lodgings and had no fixed abode in the city, they had hit upon what seemed to them a brilliant idea – that is, all three of them could be housed in the hostel they had heard the department ran for the homeless.

Linda listened courteously to this long, rambling account, trying not to recoil from the overwhelming alcoholic fumes emanating from the two labourers, and then tried to point out carefully that admission to the hostel was not a simple matter, and that the two men and their mother were not technically homeless.

This 'interview' was taking place in the corridor by the lift from which the two men had stumblingly emerged, as both interviewing rooms were already occupied. Without warning, one of the giants seized my 5 foot 1 inch tall colleague round her waist and hoisted her aloft as if she were a featherweight puppet. 'You f***ing English!' he hissed, 'you only want to look after your own. You would rather die than help the Irish!' Whereupon he all but flung her into the lift which was standing open, jabbed his thumb on the basement button and managed to sway backwards and outwards as the door was gliding shut.

This unseemly hubbub in the corridor must have penetrated the ears of those attending some kind of high-powered meeting in the chief welfare officer's office, for suddenly his door was flung wide open and he emerged. Moving as swiftly as his bulk, status and dicky ticker would permit, he approached the drama being enacted by – and now within – the lift, the deputy chief welfare officer, an ex Army major, marching in his wake. I and several other staff also abandoned our desks, and rushed in a less dignified fashion along the corridor.

By this time the lift had descended into the nether regions with the hapless Linda, leaving the two Irishmen to face the approaching posse of staff. Some quick-thinking person had evidently alerted the police, for two burly constables arrived within ten minutes to find a couple of outsize men being pinned against the wall by a dozen Lilliputians. In any scenario involving sobriety versus drunkenness, the former usually gains the upper hand eventually, especially when the alcohol intake has impeded mobility, and the two truculent construction workers were led away surprisingly meekly by the policemen. Meanwhile, Linda had managed to exit from the lift on the ground floor, very shaken but otherwise unharmed.

As we all dispersed and trooped back to our respective offices, I glanced at a large calendar on the wall. It dawned on me that today was 17 March. Perhaps on St Patrick's Day allowances should be made for inebriate behaviour by the Irish.

Fortunately, my own experience of office duty was less dramatic, but nonetheless sometimes taxing. Quite often our own clients or their relatives came to the department to see their respective social workers, and a fairly frequent visitor was a Mrs Grant, the daughter of an elderly woman who was waiting for a place in a residential home. The latter lived with her daughter and son-in-law and the domestic atmosphere was apparently electric with tension. The son-in-law and mother-in-law were no longer speaking to each other. Mrs Grant came to unburden herself to me and to try and persuade me into pushing her mother's name further up the list. All I could do was listen and murmur sympathetically, and suggest possible ways of alleviating the situation at home.

One morning she arrived and was shown into an interview room by one of the secretarial staff. After about ten minutes of the usual outpourings about her husband's hostile attitude towards her mother, she surreptitiously withdrew something from her coat pocket and placed it on the small table beside her handbag. Peering at it, I realised that it was a ten shilling note. In the mid Sixties that was no mere trifle.

'There's more where that came from,' murmured Mrs Grant. 'If you could get a place for mother in a home, I would make it worth your while.' She stroked the note enticingly with her gloved fingers. 'I expect you young women could always do with a bob or two.'

Deliberately keeping my eyes on her face and away from the money on the table, I explained quietly but firmly to Mrs Grant that we social workers were strictly forbidden to accept money from clients or their relatives. I then stood up, opened the door, and told her that I would have to bring the interview to a close as there were other calls on my time.

On another occasion as duty social worker, I was asked to interview a middle-aged man who had arrived in the department, apparently to make enquiries about help for his elderly father. It was nearly 5pm, official finishing time. The well-dressed and well-spoken man talked to me in what seemed somewhat vague terms about his father who was, it appeared, becoming quite frail. The minutes ticked by. The visitor did not seem able to come to the point of what he was trying to convey, and I began to suspect that in actual fact he really wanted to talk about something else. His vague and rambling description of his father's circumstances was probably what we called in the trade the 'presenting problem'. The real, underlying problem I was soon to discover.

Suddenly, he put his head in his hands and began to sob. Between sobs he managed to tell me that he had been made redundant that morning from his managerial post with one of Sheffield's best-known steelworks. He simply could not bring himself to go home and break the news to his wife.

Unlike today, social workers only infrequently at that time had to deal with the various ripple effects of redundancy and unemployment – financial, social and emotional. As a young, inexperienced social worker I had never before come up against a case of this nature. Perched on the hard chair in the pokey, windowless interview room, I stared in dismay at the heaving shoulders of this middle-aged man, probably old enough to be my father. What help or advice could a 24-year-old in a size ten mini dress give in these circumstances? The only sounds filtering through the door were the clank and rustle of waste bins being emptied and floors energetically polished. It was now nearly 6pm and the building would be bereft of departmental staff. No chance, therefore, of seeking advice from an older, wiser colleague.

Strangely enough, my mind did not remain blank for long. Since my mid teens I had been an enthusiastic reader of women's magazines, and I studied the problem pages with particular care and interest, sometimes mentally adding my own comments and solutions. Leaning forward, I tapped the man's arm sympathetically and suggested he should write down what had happened to him that day and hand it to his wife at a suitable moment, rather than blurting it out. Perhaps he and I could compose something together, I tentatively proposed.

Slowly he raised his head, fumbled in a trouser pocket for a handkerchief and fixed his gaze on the floor. 'Yes,' he said slowly, 'yes, we'll do that.'

Half an hour later he departed, a piece of paper, addressed to his wife, carefully folded and tucked away in his briefcase. Clearing my desk and preparing to leave myself, I reflected that Claire Rayner and Evelyn Home would have been proud of me! I clearly remembered advice such as this being proposed on one of the problem pages - when difficult news has to be broken, writing it down is sometimes less painful than verbal communication.

One in the eye for my mother, I also gleefully decided. From time to time she sarcastically expressed her disapproval of my fondness for such publications as 'Woman's Own' with remarks like 'Still reading your classics, are you?' However, I have always maintained that one is far more likely to gain insight into the personality and motives of ordinary people through studying magazines than the most diligent perusal of a so-called quality newspapers. Such an insight is invaluable for social workers.

Responsibility for homeless families also came within the remit of the Social Care Department. Following the 1977 Housing Act this responsibility was passed to housing departments, but throughout the previous decade local authority social workers employed by the welfare departments were kept busy attempting to help those unfortunates who found themselves without a roof over their heads.

Preventive work also formed part of this task. One family on my caseload came from the West Indies and were living in a rented flat. The two oldest children had been born in Trinidad, the other three in Sheffield. Their concerned GP had referred the case to us following threats of eviction from the landlord. Although the father was in work they were not managing their financial affairs very skilfully, and many debts had built up, including rent arrears. Having with difficulty persuaded the landlord to bide his time, I then tackled the daunting task of discussing with the parents ways and means of keeping within their income through thrift and disciplined budgeting.

The five children were enchanting. The youngest, a boy, was born while I was working with the family, following a pregnancy with many complications and a difficult labour. (Black babies, for some reason, I have always preferred to white babies, who seem to my eyes to resemble squashed slugs, at least when newborn.) I visited the exhausted mother in Jessop Hospital and on several occasions after she had returned home. As I sat in her small, cramped kitchen one day holding the baby while she 'mashed' tea, she suddenly and gravely announced that she and her husband had conferred together and decided that they would like to make a gift of their latest offspring to me as a mark of gratitude.

Although feeling somewhat aghast, I instinctively realised that a great honour was being bestowed upon me and that tact and circumspection must come into play when responding to this offer.

I laid the baby carefully in his carrycot in a corner of the kitchen. 'Martha,' I said slowly, 'I feel quite overwhelmed by your generous offer, but I think I shall have to say no because I live in a small attic room and I'm out at work all day.' I took a sip of tea, wondering what on earth I could say next.

'Besides,' I continued, 'I think the other kids would miss their baby brother.'

After quite a lengthy discussion along these lines, Martha, thoughtfully and in a dignified fashion, said she would withdraw her offer. This was clearly not a case of an overburdened or depressed mother trying to reject her child. Martha and Joseph doted on their children and, despite an inability to balance their own personal books, could definitely be described as good parents.

I was quite honest with them about my ignorance of West Indian culture and lifestyle. Joseph took the trouble to explain to me the difference between the traditions of the different islands. Martha came from Jamaica and shocked the health visitor one morning when the latter called. Martha had just finished bathing the baby, and was giving him a drink of dirty bath water. In response to brisk remonstrations from the health visitor, Martha attempted to point out that giving a child used bath water to drink was commonplace in her country and was believed to bring luck.

Like me, Joseph tended to be an imaginative dreamer. He described to me in vivid terms how he and his family had flown from Trinidad to Britain, never having seen the inside of an aeroplane before. An aerial view of mother earth Joseph found quite awe-inspiring, and he felt he would like to put his impressions down on paper. In fact, Joseph possessed a flair for writing and showed me some short stories he had scribbled hastily on cheap notepaper.

A considerable percentage of Afro-Caribbean and also Asian immigrants were resident in Sheffield. I considered it a privilege to work amongst them. Enoch Powell's xenophobic outbursts in 1968 directed against such immigrants, and his rabble-rousing speeches about 'rivers of blood' I found particularly distasteful. We humans reap what we sow. The arrogant British colonisation of other countries worldwide inevitably resulted eventually in many people from those countries looking to Britain for succour in economically hard times, and this we had a responsibility to respond to. Martha and Joseph were quite bewildered by Powell's diatribes, as were many immigrants I had contact with.

The couple lived in a large, shabby house which had seen better times and was divided into flats. Several times Martha mentioned a lone mother who lived on the first floor with a small child. The woman was out most of the time, including night time, and Martha suspected she earned her living as a prostitute. Martha felt uneasy about the child, who was seldom seen, and her friendly overtures to the mother were met with scarcely veiled hostility.

One morning I called to see Martha, who appeared distracted and unwilling to discuss her own affairs. She led me up the uncarpeted stairs to the first floor and paused outside a door halfway along the landing. She put her ear to the door and listened. Not a sound could be heard from the other side. 'Earlier, the little boy, he were sobbing,' whispered Martha, 'I could hear him from my living room. I'm sure he's still in there. The mother, she been out since breakfast time.'

I asked Martha if she knew whether anyone 'official' visited, such as a GP or a nurse. Martha stepped back from the door and looked at me, head on one side. 'Yes,' she said, 'a man in a uniform comes sometimes. They do call him the cruelty man.'

The door was locked but the key was in the lock on the outside. I turned it and opened the door. In the middle of a double bed sat a small boy, aged about two. His silence and inactivity were unnerving as he stared with large dark eyes at me and Martha hovering on the threshold. At that stage I knew nothing about children, but despite my ignorance I realised that no normal two-year-old should behave like this: watchful, silent, and totally motionless. The grubby room was totally unheated, and the cold was intense. It was December, shortly before Christmas, and the country had been in the grip of an icy spell for several days, with temperatures well below freezing.

I knew that I had to think and act quickly. I urged Martha to take the child down to her own warm kitchen and offer him something to eat and drink. There was no telephone in the house, so I ran outside into the street to look for a public call box. Fortunately, I soon espied one in the next street and crossed my fingers, hoping fervently that it would not have been vandalised and that the telephone directory was still intact. Luck must have been on my side for the telephone was undamaged and the book was there in its entirety. Hastily I looked up the NSPCC and dialled. Yes, they did know the child and his mother, and yes, they had started visiting following an anonymous telephone call. The inspector dealing with the child would call round immediately.

Later that afternoon, back at the office, I received a message that the little boy had been taken into care and a search had been mounted for the mother, who had still not returned.

Sometimes we were unable to prevent eviction, and sometimes cases were referred to us after eviction had taken place. Such a case represented a crisis, and mothers and children were usually admitted to our hostel. Husbands and other menfolk had to go elsewhere, many to the Salvation Army hostel. The warden who ran the hostel for mothers and their offspring was a homely woman who treated her forlorn 'flock' with compassion plus a generous dollop of brisk common sense. Her husband, who undertook odd jobs around the place, had a history of mental health problems and had been an inpatient in Middlewood. However, since the implementation of the 1959 Mental Health Act, the terms of which were in favour of patients living outside hospital as much as possible, he had been at home. His behaviour had been becoming increasingly bizarre, and we social workers were aware that his wife, and some of the inmates, were sometimes afraid of him.

One morning I arrived at work a little late as my bus had failed to turn up at the appointed time. Usually, Mr Manson, the aforementioned deputy chief welfare officer and ex-Army major, made a point of standing by the lift, watch in hand, in order to check the time of arrival of each member of staff. He was passionate about punctuality, and behaved as if he were still commanding a company. He had apparently achieved the rank of major at the age of 22 during the war, the youngest major in the history of the British Army. It would seem that this distinction had gone to his head.

Panting slightly, I erupted from the lift and braced myself for the inevitable reprimand. But Mr Manson was not in his usual position by the lift, and the long corridor was strangely quiet and deserted. I hurried along it and entered my office. The reason for the apparently deserted building immediately became clear. All the departmental staff were crowded together in this one office, some perched on the edge of desks, others leaning against the walls. In the midst of this gathering, and clearly imparting an important piece of information, stood Mr Manson, his hand resting lightly on a chair back. I slipped furtively into a corner and tried to become invisible.

There was a almost tangible air of tension in the room. My neighbour bent towards me and hissed in my ear: 'Helen's dead. Alf killed her.'

It transpired that Helen, the hostel warden, had been murdered the previous evening by her husband. He had decapitated her, and then telephoned the police and confessed to the crime. I could scarcely take in this stultifying news. Only a couple of days earlier Helen had called in at the office, and I had enquired after the welfare of a young mother and small girl I had recently taken into the hostel.

Now Helen was dead, murdered in a brutal and violent fashion, and would never again greet new arrivals, many of them traumatised themselves by tragic life histories, with a friendly pat on the shoulder and a 'Hallo, luv. Like a cuppa?'

Chapter Five

The weeks turned into months, and the months into years. I was gradually coming to the conclusion that the second half of my training needed to be undertaken. For that, I could stay in Sheffield by returning to the university there, or I could apply to the Social Studies departments at other universities for a place on their Applied Social Studies course.

The city which had initially seemed so alien when I first hesitantly set foot in its bustling midst, I had grown to love during the four years I had so far spent there. I was loath to leave it and go elsewhere. Consequently, I applied to Sheffield University for a place on their newly launched course. Following the customary completion of application forms and formal interview, I was eventually awarded a place.

Back to academia. Back to many hours spent in the university library perusing heavy tomes. Back to lengthy thesis writing. Back to the penniless status of student, and away from the relatively elevated status of employee earning a regular salary. It is hard to believe now, but in that era an attitude of respect for social workers existed amongst the general public. Social worker bashing, a popular pastime of the present day media, was virtually unknown then, and as a consequence of this, morale was generally high amongst practitioners.

I felt ambivalent about returning to a life of study and exams. The diploma I very much wanted to gain, but at the same time I was reluctant to leave my colleagues and the work I was engaged in despite the stress and the daily encounters with human pathos and conflict. Office life could be described as a microcosm of the macrocosm in that the people who form a group of workers within an office mirror the wider world outside through their interactions with each other, their gossip, jockeying for position, their petty jealousies, and mutual support when things go wrong. Just as I enjoyed observing the world from the windows of Glossop Road, so did I find the observation and being part of office life curiously satisfying. Even the good-natured teasing that sometimes came my way I knew I was going to miss. There was only one other Southerner beside myself amongst the office staff, and the two of us were dubbed soft Southerners by the Sheffielders because we balked at their attempts to cajole us into sharing their favourite lunchtime snack of chip butties and tripe!

My mother's pessimistic prophecy that I would not be liked because I was 'not one of them' had not been fulfilled. Not a single individual had shown any hostility towards me because I came from a different part of the country. In fact, I found the indigenous population spontaneously friendly and warm-hearted.

Thus it was that in September 1968 I found myself once again within the portals of the University. For a fifth year of higher education there was no chance of any kind of grant, and throughout that final year of training I lived on £4 a week, which consisted of my meagre savings plus an unexpected income tax rebate. At that time £4 went considerably further than it does now, but still the need to count every halfpenny was vital.

This time round greater importance was attached to the practical placements, and each placement lasted several months. My first was with the Children's Department. Students on this course carried a real caseload, albeit a small one, and did not merely shadow social workers. I was closely supervised, however, by an experienced child care worker, and discussed my cases with her at least twice a week.

Throughout the three years I spent with the Social Care Department I had little experience of dealing with children, apart from those I met when working with homeless families or families at risk of becoming homeless. My placement with the Children's Department consisted largely of work with prospective foster and adoptive parents, and occasionally with parents who were already fostering or had adopted a child. This was an entirely new area for me, as were the visits I paid to several children's homes.

At that time children's homes were large institutions, and children of all ages, from babies through to teenagers, were cared for under one roof. I found my visits a sobering experience. At one home the smaller children crowded round me, and one little boy, of an Asian appearance with enormous black eyes, said to me several times, 'I love you. I do love you.' In my ignorance I did not then realise that a normal child from a 'normal' background would be quite wary of a strange person and would never say 'I love you' so readily.

One couple I interviewed several times had four children of their own and decided they wished to foster. From the outset I felt there was something amiss with this family, and that their stated wish to foster actually indicated problems and conflicts which had been left hanging in the air, undealt with. It seemed significant that the mother, Mrs T, particularly wanted to foster an eight-year-old girl, the exact age of one of her own daughters who had a problem with bed-wetting, and tended to be withdrawn at home but disruptive at school. The parents always spoke in a negative fashion about this child, and it gradually became clear to me that she was the least favoured amongst their offspring. Perhaps they, in particular the mother, wanted to try and prove to themselves that they would have more 'success' with a substitute eight-year-old. Mrs T had apparently suffered from quite serious post natal depression following the birth of this daughter, and residual resentment towards her still lingered.

After six interviews I arrived at the conclusion that this couple should not become foster parents, a decision which became particularly firm when I discovered that the father was lukewarm about fostering and had been pushed by his wife into agreeing to apply. A strong gut feeling formed part of my resolve not to recommend Mr and Mrs T as prospective foster parents. Gut feelings on their own should not, needless to say, be the only factor when arriving at important conclusions, but they can sometimes be an accurate indicator.

I discussed all this in detail with my supervisor. She herself conducted a lengthy interview with the couple (as students were not permitted to deal with such intricate matters entirely by themselves), and felt that I had accurately summed up the situation. She and I then visited together to explain our decision to Mr and Mrs T. I braced myself for a hostile response. However, both seemed somehow curiously relieved. Pondering upon this afterwards, I surmised that perhaps they had been helped in some way by a thorough 'going into' of their unsatisfactory family situation, which had taught them to consider certain aspects they had never confronted before.

One family I was required to visit were already established fosterers who at the time were looking after a young boy in addition to their own two children. This six-year-old child, Michael, was posing certain problems. He was out of control at home and intimidating his classmates at school by his bullying and aggressive behaviour. The foster parents were in need of support and advice from the Children's Department.

The first time I called, Michael was shuffling across the living room floor on his knees, something dangling from his tightly clenched fist. I suppressed a gasp when I saw that the something was wriggling and was a living creature. It was in fact a small hamster. Michael appeared to be deaf to his foster mother's entreaties to put the hamster back in its cage. It apparently belonged to her own two children, and Michael refused to leave it alone. Claiming that he merely wished to play with it, he seemed on the contrary actually to take pleasure in tormenting it.

After two fairly perfunctory visits to this house, which I struggled through, I heard from the foster mother that the hamster had died. Her small daughter had come downstairs early one morning and found her pet dead in its cage, presumably pushed beyond the limits of endurance by Michael's mercilessly rough handling. I asked my supervisor if I could be taken off this case.

Abuse of animals I cannot tolerate and have never been able to work with clients of any age group who treat animals badly. To this day I feel pangs of guilt because I failed to contact the RSPCA, an organisation I had supported from early childhood, concerning this incident with the hamster.

Sometimes problems arise within adoptive families. Social workers from the Children's Department were prepared to help if approached. One such case concerned Derek, an adopted boy of 11 whose adoptive parents had recently informed him that they were not his natural parents, although they had been advised to do this when the boy was much younger. The child had not appeared to react at all to this information, indeed he had remained impassive and refused to be drawn as to his feelings on the subject. A child care worker from the department had visited several times and attempted to discuss the whole question of adoption with Derek and his parents. Derek had responded fairly well to these overtures, and was beginning to describe the shock he felt and ask questions about the circumstances surrounding his birth. My role was to carry on from here and encourage the boy to open up further.

I approached this case with little enthusiasm as I doubted whether I could establish a rapport with a child burdened with this kind of problem. However, my predecessor had clearly paved the way, for Derek seemed quite comfortable with me. At the end of my final visit, he clutched at my sleeve, his round blue eyes fixed on my face. 'I'm glad I was adopted,' he said, the words coming out in a rush. 'If my own mum had kept me, I would never have met my other mum and dad and that would have been awful.'

Only about a third of our time during this year was spent at the University in lectures and tutorials, still presided over by Eric Sainsbury. I was now mixing with an entirely new set of students, as those I had known during the first year of training had all dispersed to a variety of different jobs or training courses. This time round, because we spent the bulk of our time working within the various agencies, most of the other students became no more than acquaintances. There was one exception, however. Lynne lived in a bedsit a few hundred yards up the road at Broomhill, and she and I frequently partook of coffee in each other's abodes or went for strolls in the nearby Botanical Gardens, surely the loveliest of all public parks. Lynne became a lifelong friend, and our friendship was forged during this time spent together, when we often discussed our placements, amongst a multitude of other topics. Because Lynne hoped to become a hospital social worker, her placements were based within hospitals.

During my three years with the Social Care Department I had begun the difficult task of marrying theory to practice. This process was now continued. In seminars and discussion groups we explored how the academic study could be related to the field work we were all undertaking in child care, probation, hospital social work, the voluntary agencies, mental hospitals *et al*. I was also beginning to realise how valuable my hobby of reading from an early age had been. Some people had expressed doubts about the link between a language and literature degree and a social studies course and a career in social work. Always a reader of catholic tastes, however, it was becoming clear to me that my knowledge of literature as well as my perusal of women's magazines had provided me with an undoubted insight into human character. It could be said that literature is a mirror of actuality, of real life. I had long been fascinated by character study, and my reading of such authors as Somerset Maugham, Flaubert, Maupassant, Thomas Mann, to name but a few, had opened a window onto the causes of human behaviour and the workings of the human mind.

The year moved on quickly. My second placement I undertook with the Child and Family Guidance Service. Although my placements during the Applied Social Studies Course were both to do with work around children, this was not because I planned to specialise in any kind of child care. My type of placement and its location were determined by my financial situation which, as I have already stated, was parlous. Some students travelled outside Sheffield to undertake placements in other locations. This I could not afford to do, and my tutors kindly arranged placements for me within Sheffield, in fact within walking distance of my address in Glossop Road.

Another much appreciated 'prop' during this impecunious year were Sunday lunches consumed at the home of the aforementioned Edna and Liza Marsh, old family friends who lived in Ringinglow Road. These two ladies entertained me with stories about my great-grandmother's family who lived in a Lincolnshire village and with whom Edna and Liza and been acquainted as children in the early years of the century. Edna was also fond of impressing upon me how indebted she felt to my grandmother, who left bucolic Lincolnshire at the age of 17 and walked (yes, walked, at the end of the nineteenth century, a few years prior to Queen Victoria's death) to London to visit her sister who had taken up a teaching post in the capital. My grandmother was so entranced by the great metropolis that she never returned to the country and spent the rest of her life in London. She took under her wing the penniless and often lonely young Edna when the latter was living in London as an art student during the First World War.

At the outbreak of the second war, these two genteel and unassuming sisters, now resident in Sheffield, took into their home and their lives two German Jewish refugee children who had managed to travel to Britain with the help of the Red Cross. These girls, profoundly disturbed by their experiences in Germany, lived with Edna and Liza throughout the war years. In 1945 they learnt that their parents and most other family members had perished in Auschwitz. I was greatly moved by this story and voiced my admiration one Sunday. Liza looked at me with an expression of slight surprise on her face. 'Oh well, everyone had to do their bit, you know,' she said, 'and that was ours – our bit of war effort.'

In return, the sisters were most interested in my stories of the course and the work I was doing in different agencies. Obviously, the principle of confidentiality had to be observed, so I revealed no details such as names, and omitted some of the more earthy details of the situations I dealt with, for fear of wounding spinsterish sensibilities.

My supervisor at the child guidance clinic was a psychiatric social worker, or PSW for short, a new breed of qualified social workers to be found in psychiatric settings such as this and mental hospitals. The old style mental welfare officer, often from a military background and usually untrained, felt threatened by these, to them, alien upstarts and the resulting tension in agencies and departments where both 'old' and 'new' workers were employed sometimes created an uncomfortable atmosphere.

A wide range of childhood psychiatric disorders were dealt with by the staff at the clinic. School refusal appeared to be a common problem, and I was asked to help with some of these cases. One boy, aged about 13, I remember in particular had not been to school for two years and was receiving tuition at home. His only real interest seemed to be TV, which amounted to an infatuation, and he became totally preoccupied with the exploits of the world's first ever man on the moon during that year of 1969. This appeared to be his only topic of conversation during his sessions with me at the clinic, and it was uphill work trying to nudge him towards talking about his tribulations at home and school. This obsessive involvement with TV in general and the man on the moon in particular may have been the boy's way of evading problems which were too painful for him to face up to.

The child's mother also came to see me on several occasions. This was particularly difficult for her as she was agoraphobic, but insisted on travelling to the clinic from her home on the outskirts of the city, although I had made it clear that I was willing to visit her at home. She would arrive trembling in the office I shared with my supervisor, and tell me how, almost overcome with panic on the bus, she had alighted several stops too soon, but had found walking along the pavement almost as terrifying. This disturbed and deeply unhappy mother and son were not helped by an indifferent husband and father who had no insight into their emotional problems and refused to participate in the clinic sessions.

The clinic was presided over by Dr O, a child psychiatrist considered quite distinguished within his own profession. My experience of doctors during my time in Sheffield had been mixed. Some GPs only took an interest in their younger patients, and were of the opinion that anyone who had the effrontery to live beyond the age of 65 should be put against a wall and shot, while others went to admirable lengths to care for all their patients, including the older ones. As for hospital consultants, I had mainly come into contact with that up and coming and newly fashionable animal, the specialist in geriatric medicine. As a green 'new starter' with the Social Care department, I had one day accompanied an older colleague to the Royal Infirmary to meet Dr I, who was a big name amongst geriatricians at that time. When we arrived, he was in the middle of a ward round, sycophantic nurses and overawed students in tow.

Dr I evidently had a taste for histrionics. Having arrived at the last bed at the end of the long ward, he flung out his arms and declared to the assembled company: 'This is the dawn of a new era. Advancing years and infirmity no longer go hand in hand. Great leaps forward in medicine have started to bring about eternal youth.'

I glanced around at the pathetic bundles of aged humanity lying inert in the cot-like beds, some of them clearly in an advanced stage of senility, and reflected uneasily that Dr I was perhaps being a little over-optimistic in his vision of a rosy dawn. I had recently read Aldous Huxley's *Brave New World*, which was uncannily reminiscent of what I was witnessing in this hospital ward.

Dr O was another singular personality from the medical world. He took his duties very seriously, which included overseeing students when their supervisors were absent for any reason. At one stage mine was away ill for a period of two weeks, and Dr O actually came into the clinic, when he was officially on leave, to conduct a two-hour supervision session with me.

Those two hours were amongst the most uncomfortable I have ever yet spent. Dr O held firmly to the view that parents who treated their babies according to the theories of Truby King inevitably produced damaged and malfunctioning offspring. Truby King was a fashionable 'baby care expert' who greatly influenced parents in the Thirties and Forties and who decreed that infants should not be spoilt, should never be picked up when they cried, and should only be fed when the clock decreed. His ideas were eventually superseded by those of Benjamin Spock. Many of Dr O's patients had parents who belonged to the Truby King generation of allegedly harshly treated babies.

While I had hoped to discuss my cases, my supervision session in fact evolved into two hours of psychoanalysis after Dr O discovered, with a degree of relish, that I had been born during the war and that my mother, like thousands of other parents, had religiously followed Truby King's theories. So this was the key to my peculiarities!

Dr O treated a number of cases of anorexia and held firm views on how this illness should be dealt with. He believed that this compulsive need to be very thin was an outward manifestation of a desperate wish to return to infancy so that the sufferer could begin again at the beginning, as it were. He encouraged his anorexic patients to regress as far back as possible into babyhood. One patient, a girl of 12, who was being treated by Dr O and other staff at the clinic, I was permitted to visit at home. She had retreated into babyhood to the point where she spent most of the day in a small bed with cot sides, sucking a dummy. At intervals she allowed her mother to feed her with milk from a baby's feeding bottle. This was the only food she would agree to take. Dr O and many of his followers claimed that this controversial treatment resulted in a degree of success, but I can only say that I found the sight of this 12-year-old behaving like a helpless infant quite upsetting.

Many an anecdote concerning the patients and their life-styles were related to me by my supervisor, some of which had originally emanated from Dr O. I discovered, for example, that the young boy with school phobia and a passion for TV had been born 12 years after his parents married. It transpired that conception had not occurred because the parents were labouring under the delusion that sexual intercourse took place via the navel!

On completion of this placement there remained a lengthy thesis to write, and thereafter the course came to an end, hopefully with the award of a diploma. In due course this came my way, much to my relief. I was now a fully qualified social worker.

My five years in this proud Yorkshire city were drawing to a close. I was reluctant to leave my friends, the work, and the city, but knew this was inevitable for I was getting married and going to live in another part of Northern England.

Thus it came about that one day in August 1969 I set out on another journey into the unknown, this time to a mainly rural area, a marked contrast to my urban experience.

Chapter Six

Rain, rain, day after day of grey scudding clouds, yet more rain. I could scarcely believe that the sky could weep so many tears. In the country the weather imposed its presence upon one in a way that it never had done in my previous life in cities. In an urban setting the weather plays a relatively background role. And the wind – Westerly gales sweeping across the fields and slapping themselves, moaning and shrieking against the long-suffering house. One's umbrella blown inside out in the gale-tossed streets of Eastbury[1], discarded, and never replaced. -----shire was not a place for umbrellas, it was a place for sturdy anoraks with wind-resistant hoods, and equally tough, mud-proof wellies.

For a long time I felt acutely that I had been transported to a different planet, so great was the contrast between this new life and my previous ones. It seemed that time had been rolled back several decades. Power cuts took place with astonishing frequency. A flash of lightning or a gust of wind seemed to be enough to plunge the area into powerlessness. One of the first purchases I deemed necessary was a torch or, more fittingly, a candle.

I was shocked to discover that unpasteurised milk was still sold everywhere, for I had been brought up by a father who was one of the pioneering group of scientists in the 1930s whose

---

[1] All place names, as well as people's names, have been changed in the interests of confidentiality.

beneficial research resulted in tuberculin tested cattle and the pasteurisation of milk. Another shocking discovery was the fact that The Times newspaper could not be purchased anywhere apart from one newsagent in Eastbury. Consternation reigned the first time my mother came to stay for The Times was one of her bibles!

But above all else, the hardest thing for me to digest was the cultural diet – or rather famine. In 1969 -----shire was a cultural desert. There were, for example, no extra mural classes, only one bookshop beside WH Smith was to be found in Eastbury, and nowhere at all in the whole of the county could one purchase foreign language books. I had grown up with easy access to illustrious bookshops such as WG Foyle, where my parents regularly bought books, and throughout the eight years I had spent in two university towns I lived amidst an essentially mind-stimulating milieu. For 27 years I had taken all this for granted.

The indigenous population also seemed to belong to another country. There was not a black face to be spotted, apart from odd glimpses in Indian restaurants or amongst hospital doctors. This I found strange after mingling with so many people from ethnic minorities. The blunt, down-to-earth friendliness of the average Yorkshire person in the street did not have its counterpart in this remote rural setting. It was true that most Sheffielders looked upon Sheffield as the centre of the world, and many had never in their lives travelled more than a few miles outside the city boundaries, but nonetheless they possessed a genuine curiosity about people and places beyond their ken. On the whole, they accepted those in their midst who originated from places other than Yorkshire. Yet an essentially parochial and inward-looking attitude is perhaps to be found in all rural areas.

Eight years went by, and during this time social work played no part in my life. Two factors eventually pushed me towards a decision regarding a return to work. Firstly, I felt a growing need to seek out congenial acquaintances. Tied as I was with a toddler, I had to accept the company that was on my doorstep, so to speak, or else deprive myself and my daughter of any kind of social life. The company on my particular doorstep seemed to be preoccupied with a (to me) indigestible mixture of farming, bridge, and the organisation of Conservative Association fund-raising events. 'Are we wearing longs or shorts to Georgina's bridge party tonight?' was a typical conversation topic.

The second factor was the death of Maria Colwell in the early 1970s. Listening to radio and TV commentaries and reading newspaper reports about the tragic death of this child, I gradually became aware that public attitudes towards the social work profession were shifting. Social workers were fast becoming the 'baddies' of society, people who allowed the death of an innocent child. Throughout the next 25 years, as one child death after another became front page news, social workers were portrayed in the media as ogres, almost as if they, rather than the actual perpetrators, had murdered the children.

In the aftermath of the Maria Colwell scandal I began to reflect more and more on the work that I had left behind in Sheffield. What had happened to the profession that I had reluctantly entered but had grown to appreciate and feel a loyalty towards? Yes, undoubtedly there was sometimes incompetence, bungling, sloth, and lack of communication which played a part in the headline-hitting scandals; but I knew there was another side to the profession. I felt the time had come to rediscover my own world.

At the age of five, my daughter started full-time school, and I decided to take the plunge and apply for a temporary social work post at the local general hospital in Eastbury, being advertised in the local paper. I and another applicant both wanted to work part-time because of family commitments, and the powers-that-be decided to appoint both of us on a part-time basis.

Again, I felt the clock had been put back some years. Feeling very nervous as I had been out of the world of work for some time, I had to pluck up considerable courage to venture onto the wards and talk to patients and their relatives. The fact that we social workers were obliged to wear white coats, which tended to confuse patients and staff alike, did not help to allay my feelings of uncertainty. During my hospital placements almoners, as hospital social workers were still called, did not have to don white coats. The terminology had now been updated to 'medical social worker', but everything else seemed somewhat outdated. This was probably largely because the principal social worker in charge of the team, Miss S, was one of the old school. One could sense the air of conflict between her and some of her older team members, and the younger, more go-ahead staff with different ideas.

My white coat caused some patients to feel convinced that I was a doctor. Indeed it was difficult trying to persuade one or two that I was no such thing. One elderly man insisted on describing his various illnesses to me in minute detail, and demanding a precise diagnosis and prognosis, when I was in fact endeavouring to discuss his home circumstances. Eventually, when no diagnosis was forthcoming, he looked at me in disgust, sat bolt upright in bed with two strands of hair carefully smoothed across his otherwise bald pate, and pronounced, 'That's what comes of allowing lasses to become doctors. It's a man's job. You should be at home in your kitchen.' So much for the hard-won advances of the feminists throughout the century!

Shedding my hated white coat seemed to be the only solution. Before entering a ward I would quickly slip off the coat and stuff it behind any convenient piece of furniture which presented itself, hoping as I did so that Miss S would not suddenly materialise. Having done that, I could then, metaphorically speaking, don my own identity, that of social worker, and sally forth to listen to and discuss a myriad social and emotional problems with anxious patients.

The work I and my fellow temporary colleague undertook was focused on the geriatric wards, as they were then still called. Talking to patients on the wards and to relatives when they visited was familiar to me and reminded me of similar experiences in the Sheffield hospitals. However, sometimes I visited relatives at home and carried out follow-up visits to patients after discharge. Some of these lived in remote villages or isolated cottages and farms, and travelling to these rural outposts was a novel experience for me. By this time I could drive, and had even passed my test first time, but I suspect that this was because I was seven months pregnant at the time, and so large that I had difficulty fitting myself in behind the wheel. The examiner seemed quite wary of me. Perhaps he feared I would give birth during the test, and then he and I would both have to grapple with quite a different kind of 'testing time'. The test completed, he leapt hurriedly out of the car like a coiled spring suddenly released, muttering over his shoulder that I had passed and he was on his way to speak to my instructor.

Although I was now a qualified driver, driving could scarcely be described as my favourite occupation, particularly in adverse weather conditions. Throughout the winter of 1977 there were several cold snaps. It was during one such wintry spell that I was obliged to visit an elderly couple in a hamlet between Eastbury and Benton. A few snowflakes were twirling casually from a grim, grey sky as I drove out of the hospital car park. By the time I had reached the outer suburbs of Eastbury and was heading into the open country, the occasional snowflake had become a blizzard and visibility was virtually nil. Somehow I struggled on, squinting at scarcely legible signposts, until I realised that I was totally lost.

Panic set in. I had a vision of myself and my car being buried underneath mountains of snow, and my small daughter waiting in vain outside the school gates for a mother who never arrived. I managed to clamber out of the car onto the narrow, snowy road and extricate the boots that I always kept in the car, just in case, from the recesses of the boot. Pulling these on, I glanced around me. The only sign of life was a number of sheep, huddled by a hedge and regarding me with frank curiosity. At least the snow appeared to have stopped for the time being, and the sky was a lighter shade of grey.

What should I do? I decided to try and make my way to the nearest habitation and ask for directions. Trudging through the snow for about half a mile, I caught sight of some farm buildings nestling in a hollow and directed my labouring footsteps to the farmhouse. A woman of ample proportions came to the door. I explained my predicament and asked her if she could point the way to Mr and Mrs D's house. Glancing at my watch, I wondered if in fact there was time for this home visit. It was now midday.

'Mr and Mrs D? Oh yes,' replied the Amazonian lady, who I took to be the farmer's wife, 'they live yonder, a mile up the hill', and she waved her plump hand in an easterly direction. I wondered vaguely how on earth I was going to coax my car up a snow-covered hill and then down again when the woman suddenly said, 'If you'll 'bide a minute, Dan will take you.' Whereupon she stepped outside and hollered in a stentorian voice for Dan. A very small, jockey-like man, as slight as his wife was substantial, appeared round the corner of the house.

Thanking them both profusely, I expected Dan to lead me to his car, but after following him across a yard and into a ramshackle barn, all I could see was a dirty red tractor with a kind of box attached to the back of it. 'Jump in lass,' invited

Dan, indicating the box. 'This'll get you up the hill.'

Fifteen minutes later and we had arrived at my clients' cottage. They did not seem at all fazed by the sight of their social worker arriving in such an undignified fashion, crouched in a receptacle commonly used to transport individual lambs and ewes on the back of a tractor.

Kindly Dan fetched me a little later, and trundled me in similar fashion back down the hill. I was glad to see the snowstorm had still not resumed, although the entire landscape, including the road, was overlaid by an inch or two of glistening white down. Dan even went so far as to drive my car back to the main road which, although fairly treacherous, was passable. Yet another notch to place on the string of novel experiences I had so far encountered in my social work career. This rural adventure was a foretaste of things to come in future years.

Hospital consultants usually look upon themselves as the gods of the medical world, and the two geriatricians in charge of the geriatric wards at the Infirmary were no exception. Dr F was renowned and revered in geriatrician circles. Towards his elderly patients, with whom he was undeniably popular, he possessed a distinct bedside manner, but held the staff under him in thrall. Some of the young doctors lived in fear of him, and I personally witnessed one raw young houseman reduced to tears following a scathing admonition from the great man. This painful scene took place in front of several people, and the humiliation must have been intense. Social workers Dr F looked upon as some kind of subspecies.

Dr B possessed a quintessentially courteous manner. He would listen quietly and in a gentlemanly fashion while I or one of my colleagues explained as persuasively as possible why we thought such and such a patient should remain in hospital for a while longer or why he should be allowed to return to his own home rather than be admitted to residential care against his will. Dr B would then reiterate his own decision regarding the matter as a foregone conclusion, as if I or the other person had never spoken. No one ever budged him once he had decided what was best for a patient.

The social work team at the hospital were a pleasure to work with. I had been outside this type of world for so long that I had almost forgotten what it was like to engage in lively discussions over coffee on social work issues and related topics such as alcoholism or marital breakdown, for example, not to mention less weighty subjects like the price of children's shoes or the ghastliness of parents' evenings. The team members were most welcoming and friendly towards me and my other half, and I began to regret that this was not a long-term post.

The six months were soon over, and at the end of July 1977 I bade everyone a reluctant goodbye. Another 16 months were to go by before I once again found gainful employment.

Chapter Seven

I was cooking fish fingers for my daughter's tea when the telephone added its intrusive tone to the sound of sizzling fat. Wondering for the hundredth time why people always telephoned at the most inconvenient moments, I pushed the pan off the ring and lifted the receiver. A male voice introduced himself as the team leader at Fairfield Social Services department. 'I have your name on a list of qualified social workers in the area who are available for work,' he went on to explain. 'We could offer you seven hours a week.'

Seven hours a week, I reflected. That would be slightly less than one full day or two mornings per week. Part-time work I was certainly looking for, but this was the leanest part-time I had ever heard of. Was it worth it?

A day or two later I rang back to say I would like to accept the post, and it was agreed that I would start in two weeks' time, at the end of November 1978, following an interview held at the Fairfield office. In the interim I had come to the conclusion that working seven hours a week, although scarcely enough time to take on a proper caseload, would represent a foot in the door. It might lead to better things.

Several years earlier local authorities had undergone a reorganisation and the separate local authority social work agencies had disappeared. Seebohm's vision of one integrated social work department meeting the needs of all vulnerable people, be they children, the elderly, people with mental health problems, the physically handicapped, or the mentally handicapped, under one umbrella, had come to fruition. The era of the social services department had begun. Each social worker employed therein should in theory be able to deal with every aspect of professional social work. It remained to be seen how this utopian ideal would work in the long-term when translated into the harsh, real world.

Fairfield is a small market town 11 miles from Eastbury. At the time, when I first took up my post in this town, the department was a small sub-office, the main area office being some 20 miles further west. The team consisted of ten social workers, a welfare assistant and a team leader, supported by two secretarial staff, and we were situated on the first floor of the flat-roofed council offices.

Due to the ill-fitting windows, we were assailed by icy blasts in the winter, a particular trial for those unfortunates whose desks were placed near the windows, and in the summer, if the temperature ever exceeded 65°F (in -----shire this is not, fortunately, a common occurrence), the atmosphere inside the office resembled that of a sauna as a direct result of the flat roof. An unsatisfactory working environment can seriously affect the standard of work undertaken by employees, so please take note, all sanctimonious critics of social workers and unthinking architects of office buildings. Next time foster parents run away with the foster children entrusted to their care, or an elderly person who is a client of the local social services department is found stiff as a board from hypothermia on her living room floor, please pause and reflect. The social workers dealing with those cases may have had to write their reports and make their telephone calls sitting in a noisy, open plan office in a freezing draught or a headache-inducing tropical heatwave. I say this only partly tongue-in-cheek.

I was interviewed by the team leader and two other staff from the managerial ranks. As I was ushered through the main office to the team leader's office, I was aware of curious eyes following me. For the interview I had decided to don a dark grey trouser suit, and it suddenly occurred to me as I walked past a number of people that I probably bore a strong resemblance to a bus conductress.

The three men who interviewed me seemed highly amused on hearing that my salary in Sheffield, as a full-time worker, amounted to the princely sum of £820 per annum. By 1978 wages and salaries had risen somewhat, but social workers were still poorly paid in comparison with many other professional people. A relatively substantial pay rise came about several years later.

I must have passed muster during this interview, for the team leader, Geoff, launched into a fairly detailed description of the work undertaken by the team and mentioned several cases he felt I could tackle. This was a 'generic' team – that is, every type of social problem besetting all client groups was dealt with, thus embodying the Seebohm-induced philosophy of a comprehensive approach to social work rather than concentrating on specialist areas.

It transpired that Geoff had also done his social work training in Sheffield, although a few years later than mine. We reminisced about the city, the university staff, and the social work placements. Earlier in the interview I had described my varied experiences as regards student placements, and Geoff remarked that such a variety of experience would undoubtedly prove invaluable when working within a generic team. He outlined the work undertaken in the field of childminder registrations, pre-school playgroup inspection and registration, fostering and adoption, child protection (although this term was not yet in use), work with the elderly comprising residential care, day care, meals-on-wheels, and care at home, a range of services used to help the physically and mentally handicapped (some time later the terminology changed to 'people with learning difficulties or disabilities'), and also work with clients of all ages suffering from mental health problems.

After the interview and subsequent discussion, I was invited to meet my future colleagues. Not all were in the office, of course. As is the nature of social work, some were out visiting clients or attending meetings. A few days later when I eventually started work, bit by bit I met the rest. The team was made up of a pleasing balance of male and female staff, ranging in age from mid 20s to late 50s. I was aged 36 at the time, so fitted neatly into the age range.

On that grey November day, as I sat at the desk assigned to me and looked around at my colleagues, all strangers as yet, I wondered how on earth I would succeed in carrying out even a fraction of the work of the department in seven hours per week, let alone gain experience in every area.

Little did I know then that I would spend the next ten years at the Fairfield office and come into contact with virtually every type of case and problem known to the world of social work!

Chapter Eight

For the first three years I worked two mornings per week, and cases that could be suitably slotted into this very limited time had to be carefully selected. Geoff, the team leader, was of the opinion that I should try my hand at interviewing people who wished to become registered childminders. This involved talking to applicants in their own homes, impressing upon them the importance of police checks amongst other factors, and also looking carefully at the home itself, for the environment where children would spend their day was of great importance. I also took part in the routine inspection of playgroups, a tumultuous undertaking during which I and the playgroup leader shouted hoarsely at each other above the infantile hubbub.

My colleague, Margaret, had been a social worker at Fairfield for several years before I arrived on the scene, and had become quite involved in the childminding registration business. I discovered that Margaret was employed for 30 hours per week and that my seven added to her 30 equalled one full-time post. Thus the office achieved its full quota of staff, and I was enlightened as to why I had been asked to work such a strange number of hours. Over the next eight years Margaret and I responded to the bulk of the childminder applications until she was obliged to retire early due to ill-health. For the remaining two years of my stint with Fairfield Social Services, I plodded on alone. We both, of course, carried a varied caseload which included many clients other than childminders.

Between us Margaret and I devised an information booklet for would-be childminders which some artistic friends of mine skilfully illustrated. This gave answers to questions such as what to do if a child became ill during the day, safety rules to be observed in the home, for example providing a suitable fireguard, and how to behave towards the children's parents. Today, -----shire Social Services Department is awash with booklets covering every aspect of departmental business, but in the late Seventies and early Eighties I was acutely aware of – and puzzled by – the lack of information available to the general public. Margaret and I therefore regarded ourselves as pioneers in this field and we proudly had printed a substantial number of booklets which were quite widely used in our local authority until some of the information contained therein became out of date following the 1989 Children Act.

A steady trickle of childminding applications found their way into the Fairfield office, as did enquiries from parents looking for childminders. Many mothers wanted or needed to work and were obliged to make proper arrangements for the care of their children. Some left their children with grandparents or other relatives, but by this stage of the twentieth century, many grandparents were working themselves and unable to fit care of grandchildren into their busy schedules.

Over the years a considerable amount of nonsense has been both written and spoken on the subject of working mothers. As long as a child is looked after in a consistent fashion by a caring and responsible adult, it matters not one iota whether that adult is a parent or an appropriate substitute such as a good childminder. In my experience, many childminders are better at the parenting role than the parents themselves. After all, they choose to become childminders because of a particular interest in young children; the same can't be said for all parents!

Due to the criticism and disapproval prevalent in Western society that has been levied at mothers who work outside the home, these women hump around with them an ever present burden of guilt like a sack of potatoes. In some cultures it is the norm for all women to work, unless handicapped or aged, and children are cared for in nurseries from earliest babyhood. No millstone of guilt there.

The bulk of the work I carried out in connection with childminding applications was essentially routine, but from time to time problems arose unexpectedly which had to be tackled. Occasionally a conflict developed between a parent (usually the mother) and the childminder. This often originated from complex feelings of guilt and jealousy on the part of the mother. One such mother I dealt with vigorously objected to everything the childminder did with her small son. Both took to telephoning me at the office to complain about each other. Eventually I agreed to meet them at the childminder's house to try and sort out the dispute *tête à tête*.

I arrived to find a slanging match already well underway with four young children seated on the floor amidst a sea of toys or gleefully using the sofa as a trampoline, unheeded by the baleful grown ups.

'You will *not* give George beefburgers and chips for his dinner! I don't want him eating such rubbishy food! He's to have salad and scrambled egg.' George's mother, somewhat startlingly attired in sunset-red leggings straining to cover her ample bottom, and a red and orange beret topped by a large black pompom, emphasised her point by banging her imposing canvas handbag against the side of the sofa.

The childminder, Maureen, ran her hand through what there was of her cropped hair, while the aforementioned George, amply built like his mother, zoomed a battered toy tractor expertly round and round Maureen's jean-clad ankles.

'But I tried giving him salad and that and he wouldn't eat a thing. He threw the lettuce on the floor and then threw himself after it and screamed until I offered him a sausage.' Maureen's irritation was clearly contained with difficulty.

Suddenly George's mother lunged forward and seized the silver chain which was dangling round Maureen's neck. Dropping the canvas bag, she violently pushed Maureen backwards; the childminder tripped over a piece of Lego and banged her head on the tall bookcase by the door. George's mother tightened her grip on the necklace and began furiously shaking Maureen as if she were a muddy doormat. The two little girls happily bouncing on the sofa/trampoline stopped in mid-bounce, mouths agape, to watch this fascinating adult spectacle. It was better than the telly any day!

At this juncture I decided physical intervention was a necessary solution. Delicate social work skills such as diplomacy, negotiation and patient reasoning were clearly inappropriate. Stepping smartly forwards, I seized George's mother by the wrist, digging my nails slightly into the flesh. Startled by this unexpected move on the part of the social worker whose more conventional role is to listen, empathise and discuss, she let go of the silver chain and stumbled backwards. I planted myself firmly between the two women and declared in a no-nonsense voice that fisticuffs simply could not be tolerated.

The outcome of this drama was to provide George and his mother with a different childminder. This was not altogether successful as the mother continued to be critical of the way her child was handled, but at least the two women did not lock horns. I exchanged a discreet word with George's health visitor, who engaged George's mother in a tactful discussion about the benefits of a reasonably relaxed yet still healthy approach to nutrition and other matters of child rearing.

After a year or two I started working somewhat longer hours and was able to take on a more complex caseload.

Preventive and supervisory work with children was considered to be of prime importance. The phrase 'child protection' had not yet crept into the terminology; baby battering was, however, a popular expression, much in vogue amongst all branches of the media.

One case I became involved with comprised two children aged six and four and their parents, who had recently split up. The father himself had come to the office to ask for help at the request of a concerned housing visitor. A matrimonial supervision order was eventually placed on the family which meant in effect that the children would be supervised by the Social Services until they attained the age of 18. This was not the first or the only case of its kind that I experienced, but it stands out in my long journey through a social work career because of its unique characteristics, and because I fell into the dangerous trap of becoming over-involved.

The father, Frank, a pint-sized man with a diffident air, had had an injunction taken out against him shortly before he asked for our help, banning him from the matrimonial home, a council house in Fairfield. Domestic violence was the allegation; his wife Joanne claimed he routinely and brutally assaulted her.

Over the succeeding weeks and months, as I gradually became acquainted with the situation and with the people involved in it, I grew convinced that Joanne was in fact the violent one, and it was she who routinely assaulted Frank. She was a tall, strapping young woman with an overbearing manner, and, as I was soon to discover, an alarmingly distorted and man-eating personality. Men are not the sole perpetrators of violence within the home, believe me.

Carl and Karen, the two children, were as different as junket from roast boar. At the age of four, Karen was already showing signs of becoming a replica of her mother: bold and brash, she shouted loudly if thwarted, while Carl was quiet and wary with the same timid air as his father. As I observed the two children interacting with their mother, it soon became clear to me that Carl was afraid of Joanne.

The health visitor was not satisfied with the way the children were being cared for. There was much gossip in the neighbourhood about Joanne's wild behaviour, and the fact that she spent every evening out with a multitude of different men, frequently leaving the children unattended. Frank maintained that his estranged wife was not fit to look after the children and endeavoured to have them stay with him in his rented cottage in an isolated village as often as possible. This proved difficult, however, as Joanne often refused to let the children go to their father. Joanne's mother played a dominant role in this scenario – dominant being a key word as, like her daughter, she was a large, imposing woman with a forceful, almost bullying manner, much given to wearing swirling cloaks. She owned and ran a private residential home for the elderly in Eastbury and speculation was rife in the office as to how the residents were treated by this female Dracula.

It was she who had employed and paid a solicitor to serve an injunction against Frank. She sometimes had the children to stay at weekends and was openly critical of the way her daughter dealt with the children. It seemed to me that she wished to alienate both parents and take over the children herself. She was also critical of my attempts to keep father and offspring in touch with each other, which I considered to be of great importance.

Because of concerns expressed in various quarters about Joanne's neglect of the children, particularly at night, from time to time I took to sitting in my car in the evening near Joanne's house. Each time I did this I witnessed Joanne leaving the house. I began to feel more like a detective than a social worker, and was uncomfortably aware that this case was beginning to play too big a part in my life. My nocturnal vigils came to an end when one evening, as I prepared to drive away from Joanne's house, the ignition key snapped in two as I tried to start the engine. A frantic call home from a public call box resulted in my husband being obliged to drive out to rescue me, complete with small daughter wrapped in a blanket on the back seat, having been plucked, protesting, from her warm bed. Unlike Joanne, we did not leave a young child alone in the house.

By this time it was about 10pm on a frosty November night. As I sat waiting in my car, almost paralysed with cold, Joanne and a man suddenly came into view in the light of a street lamp, walking towards me. My attempts to become invisible by pulling my scarf across my mouth and crouching down as far as possible behind the steering wheel were to no avail. Joanne recognised my car and me as she drew nearer, and a few swift strides brought her face on a level with mine.

'Spying again, are you?' she whooped in a carrying contralto, while her male companion, a lanky beanpole, hovered a foot or so behind her. 'I've seen you on a night, lying in wait to see if you can catch me out. What I do or don't do with my kids is not your bloody business!' Whereupon she yanked open the car door, which I had foolishly omitted to lock from the inside, and grasped my arm with the obvious intent of pulling me out onto the pavement. In the ensuing struggle I managed to pull the door sharply to again, and in doing so accidentally trapped Joanne's arm. She let forth a screech of rage and pain which must have been audible in the next county, and started hurling invectives at me and my car. Throughout this, Mr Beanpole perched himself on a garden wall and feebly echoed Joanne's imprecations.

Living room curtains were pulled back, lights snapped on, and people appeared at their garden gates, curious and perplexed by the commotion. Trying to make myself heard above the hubbub, I became aware of a car turning into the street at the far end. It was hubby driving straight into a scene reminiscent of a street brawl from a film!

Not long after this, Joanne's formidable mother came sweeping into the office one afternoon, cloak whirling importantly round her shoulders, to lodge a complaint against me with my team leader. She not only objected to the 'spying episode', but maintained that I was a liar because I upheld Frank's claim that Carl was regularly physically abused by his mother. Carl quite frequently had bruising on his body that could not be explained away, and which staff at his infants school had noticed and reported to us. It was clear that Joanne disliked her small son and that his attitude towards her was one of a wary animal.

Frank applied for custody of the children, but the court turned down the application because he refused to give up his job and look after the children while living on benefits instead. Poor Frank; he had lost his children, his home, and his wife (astonishingly, he consistently claimed that he still loved Joanne), and consequently he clung tenaciously to the one big factor in his life that had not slipped from his grasp, that is, his work as a welder. In my report to the court, I emphasised the fact that Frank's parents were able and willing to take the children to and from school etc, but all to no avail. I felt convinced that he was the more stable of the two parents and that the children would have benefited from living with him.

Carl in particular worried me. A withdrawn child who said little, he was nonetheless clearly attached to his father. One morning I paid a brief visit to his school to explain to Carl and his sister that I was trying to arrange for them to spend weekends at their father's cottage. Carl gazed out of the window, then turned back to me. Raising sad brown eyes to mine he said awkwardly, 'When you next see my dad, can you tell him I love him?'

Eventually Joanne left Fairfield and moved with the children to Eastbury, 11 miles away, no doubt thinking she could throw off the shackles of the Social Services department by so doing. Not so. A supervision order remained applicable wherever the children happened to be. The case was reallocated to a young Irish social worker, Sean, who had recently started working with Eastbury Social Services. At first all appeared satisfactory. Sean and I exchanged a few telephone calls in order to discuss the case, and I called in at the Eastbury office to hand over the file. It was shortly after this that strange rumours began to circulate about Sean. He had been spotted several times in the evening in various venues in Eastbury dressed as a woman and heavily made up. In the early 1980s, this kind of behaviour in a small, provincial town like Eastbury was still kept under wraps. Boy George had not yet burst upon the scene!

Sean was eventually unmasked as an impostor – that is, it came to light that he was not a qualified social worker as he had maintained at the job interview and that his degree and other certificates had been forged. He claimed to be a graduate of the University of Eire. There is, of course, no such seat of learning, and the foolishness and ignorance of Social Services senior managers can scarcely be credited. They were taken in by this subterfuge, and no checks were carried out on Sean's credentials.

He was dismissed from his post under a cloud when this and another equally serious misdemeanour were discovered. He was found guilty of that taboo of all taboos where social workers and clients are concerned – he became involved in a sexual relationship with Joanne, who started openly bragging about it in local pubs and nightclubs. When questioned about this, Sean quite readily admitted to it. Sean and his exploits and deceits provided Social Services personnel with an absorbing topic of gossip for months.

This sad and unsatisfactory case left its mark on me. I learnt much from it, not least that social workers are ill advised to become too involved with any one case. Patrick, one of my colleagues with many years' experience of complex work with children, gave me some sound advice: 'Always be on your guard against getting sucked into a situation, and remember that you can't spend an inordinate amount of time on one case, otherwise your other cases will suffer.' I have always heeded those wise words.

It might seem from what I have depicted so far of my cases involving children that life at work was one long round of vigorous manhandling and getting physical. However, this was not the case. Two of my cases where I worked with dysfunctional families contained the demon drink as the principal ingredient. Ben was a child of seven when I first met him; he had been born with cerebral palsy. His mother, Sally, had a serious drink problem and was wedded not only to her husband, Jake, but also to the sherry bottle. She would spend hours scuttling furtively in and out of all the local supermarkets in search of the cheapest cooking sherry on offer.

Sally was already hooked on drink at the time of Ben's birth and doctors suspected that the alcohol had contributed to his handicaps. He attended a special school in Eastbury and was conveyed there and back by taxi. On quite a few occasions the taxi driver was loath to drop him off because of the situation that was only too apparent inside the house. No Sally would appear at the back door to greet her son. Ben and the taxi driver would push the door open and go inside. Sometimes she was so drunk that she did not recognise her own child, and on one occasion Ben stumbled over her lying unconscious in the hall. Occasionally Ben was brought to the Council offices round the corner where one of us would 'mind' him until his mother was in a fit state to take over.

Yet when Sally was sober she enjoyed being a mother. She was also basically quite domesticated and took an interest in cookery. In her more honest moments, she maintained she would like to overcome her dependence on booze, but her motivation was never quite strong enough to achieve this aim. I arranged for her GP to hold regular counselling sessions with her, but this was totally unsuccessful as the doctor stuck to the customary ten minutes allotted to each patient, and by the time the ten minutes were up, Sally had scarcely plucked up courage to open her mouth.

Doctors clearly made Sally feel jittery. At regular intervals Ben had appointments to see a paediatrician in Eastbury so that the latter could monitor his development. As Sally had a tendency to miss these appointments, I opted to convey her and Ben to the hospital. While waiting to see the consultant, Sally would disappear quite frequently, ostensibly to visit the Ladies. After each absence she became visibly more intoxicated until she was lurching, rather than walking, back into the waiting room. She confessed that nervousness and apprehension over what the doctor might pronounce concerning Ben's progress, or lack of it, drove her to take secret swigs from a bottle of sherry hidden in her large shopping bag. This doubtless provided the other occupants of the waiting room with some memorable entertainment, but scarcely enabled Sally to take in what the doctor had to say.

Taking Sally to Turning Point in a nearby town was a venture which might have succeeded, but she drew back at the last moment. Turning Point is an organisation set up to help people addicted to drugs and alcohol. Those who apply for help and are accepted are obliged to live for a number of weeks in the Turning Point hostel while they receive individual counselling and group therapy. I drove Sally there several times, and she clearly liked the staff and the whole set-up. But staying in the hostel would have meant separation from

Ben and all the attendant problems of arranging for him to be looked after. Eventually Sally backed down, and another attempt to find a solution bit the dust.

Matters finally came to a head one evening in my presence. I had arranged to see Sally and Jake together at home. Ben was away, spending a week in a respite care home in Eastbury. In a stormy atmosphere, full of accusations, bitterness and hostility on the part of both husband and wife, Jake and Sally took to hurling insults at each other. I suspected that this was a new experience for them and that only superficial communication ever took place between them. After the bitter phase had exhausted itself, they became calmer and started a more rational dialogue, with me acting as referee.

Not long after this I closed the case. Sally was still drinking, but was making genuine efforts to curb her alcohol consumption. She had also responded to suggestions that she try and develop interests which would perhaps take the place of sherry in her life. She started cooking more and setting aside 'fun time' for Ben. Jake reacted positively by spending more time with his family. Not a totally successful outcome to my involvement with the case, but 'success' in social work is elusively difficult to measure. Other individuals and agencies were keeping a watchful eye on Ben's welfare: the staff at his school, his GP, and the nurses and care assistants who ran the respite care home. I knew that if they were unduly concerned our department would be notified.

An almost complete lack of success manifested itself when I tackled another 'drink' case. The scenario here comprised Fran, a single mother with two teenage daughters by different men, and the girls' grandmother. Obvious collusion had been taking place between the two women for some time, though the grandmother claimed total ignorance of her daughter's over fondness for gin. This was difficult to credit in view of the fact that Fran kept her supply of gin bottles in the spin dryer which was regularly used by all the family!

The teaching staff at the local comprehensive school where both girls were pupils referred the case to our department because of grave concerns over their lifestyle, which the staff felt was generated by Fran's drinking. The girls were themselves drinking and had also been heavy smokers for several years, a particular problem where the younger girl was concerned because she was severely asthmatic. The older girl had become a mother herself recently but did not show much interest in the baby.

Fran maintained that she was motivated to fight her dependence on gin, and fell in with my arrangements for her to see a counsellor from a local drug and alcohol rehabilitation unit. The counselling sessions took place in the Social Services office. After a few weeks I allowed myself a cautious pat on the back, metaphorically speaking. Fran kept all the appointments, talked freely to the counsellor and, most important of all, always arrived sober.

However, it transpired that she was pulling the wool over the eyes of all of us. One afternoon I emerged from a client's house on the same estate where Fran and co lived. Just as I was about to unlock my car door, I spotted a stout figure rather unsteadily wheeling a pram along the pavement 50 yards away. Fran! As I gazed, one hand on the car door, Fran fumbled clumsily underneath the pram cover, whipped out a bottle and took a swig from it. Then she replaced the screw top, and tucked the bottle out of sight again.

The elderly man tending his garden next door paused from his labours. Pointing his trowel in Fran's direction, he said in a sorrowful voice: 'She's a cunning 'un, that. She goes to see that welfare lady in the council offices every week nice and sober, then she comes out and goes straight into the Co-op and buys gin and drinks while she's taking grandbabby out.'

So much for all our efforts. I was beginning to discover not only how insidious are the effects of alcohol abuse on all the members of a family, but how difficult it is to find a satisfactory solution to addiction.

Chapter Nine

The word 'generic' is misleading when applied to a social work team. Most social workers who belong to such a team discover after a year or two where their interests really lie and start concentrating on one or two client groups. Thus a generic team consists in actual fact of a group of specialists working together in perhaps one large open plan office, or two or three smaller ones under the same roof.

As in Sheffield, my colleagues in Fairfield were a motley assortment. Apart from Patrick, the Irishman with a seductive Dublin accent, who refused to work with any group other than children, there were Bill and Vernon, both of whom had a substantial number of elderly clients on their caseload. Vernon had also been working with people with mental health problems for many years and sometimes, as duty social worker, he was called out at night to deal with situations that were frequently bizarre and occasionally quite dangerous. He entertained us with many an anecdote: for example, the evening he spent trekking for miles over the hills, armed police bringing up the rear, in hot pursuit of a man with an acute psychotic illness who was convinced he possessed the ability to fly and had been given a divine mission to take off from the top of a mountain. Vernon eventually persuaded him to go to hospital on a voluntary basis by bribing him with the possibility of floating into the ether from the hospital roof!

Posterity was unfortunately not informed as to whether he ever accomplished this feat.

Out-of-hours emergency duty was something in which I fortunately did not have to take part. Only full-time staff were on this rota. It was not only Vernon who had unlikely experiences to recount. Marina, another social worker who, like Patrick, tended to specialise in children's cases, was involved one August night in a dark and lengthy hike across fields to an isolated cottage where an elderly woman lived alone. Because she was unused to dealing with this client group, Marina telephoned Kath, the home care officer responsible for organising home care assistance for those who needed it, in order to discuss the situation, and Kath suggested they ventured forth together to this elderly person's house. She had been there before and knew the way.

Apparently a very young and newly recruited home care assistant had visited this client earlier in the day and found her most unwell. Later in the evening the young girl blurted out her concerns to her aunt, also a home care assistant. The latter, feeling somewhat dismayed because her young niece had failed to notify either the GP or the home care officer, decided the situation was sufficiently serious to warrant alerting the duty social worker.

The cottage was situated about two miles away from the nearest road and could only be approached on foot across fields. By the time Kath and Marina met up in the lay-by where they left their cars, it was nearly midnight. Armed with two torches they set off over the first field. The sky was overcast and the darkness total. It was also very still and even the slightest sound could be heard with crystal clarity. What was that sudden heavy breathing, that sound of feet splodging through mud and coming nearer? Kath and Marina gripped their torches tightly and forged onwards, concentrating on reaching the gate at the far end of the field. Suddenly they were surrounded by large, lumbering shapes jostling one another and bumping against the two women, who uttered little shrieks and began to clamber over the gate. A group of cows, most curious about this nocturnal intrusion, were left milling around by the gate, staring after Kath and Marina and snorting excitedly through their nostrils.

Fortunately there were no livestock in the second field. Once through that and over another gate the final stretch of the expedition consisted of a walk or, more accurately, a stumbling trot, along a lane bordered by trees on both sides. This was particularly spooky as the quiet night air seemed full of sudden rustlings, flapping noises and weird cries as birds and other small creatures moved about in the undergrowth and foliage.

At the far end of the winding lane the torches lit up the elderly woman's little cottage, in total darkness, the curtains undrawn.

'You go round to the back and see if you can get in the back door, while I knock on the front door,' whispered Kath to Marina.

Marina felt her way round the side of the house, falling over broken flower pots and a clothes prop as she did so. However, the back door was securely fastened. Kath was having no more luck round at the front. Her sharp taps with the large brass knocker met with silence. She shone the beam of her torch onto her watch – 1.20am.

'We'll have to go down the road to Meadowland Farm,' she announced to Marina whose shadowy figure re-appeared from the back garden. 'The farmer keeps a spare key to Betty's cottage.'

Half a mile further down the narrow lane they found themselves at the farm, also in total darkness. A dog started barking furiously as they searched for the farmhouse amongst the jumble of outbuildings. Brisk raps on the front door brought no response.

Kath bent down in a determined fashion and scooped up a handful of gravel and small stones from the front path. Without more ado, she hurled them upwards in the direction of what she hoped was a bedroom window, curtains firmly drawn. The stones rattled furiously against the glass, and suddenly the house sprang to life. Lights went on, windows were thrown up, and footsteps could be heard on stairs.

Farmer Bell appeared at the door after much turning of keys and shooting of bolts. Gaping in astonishment, he listened to my colleagues' apologies for the disturbance, and explanations as to why they needed a key to Betty's house.

'That Betty Holbrook, she shouldn't be living on her own like that,' he muttered as he threw a coat on over his pyjamas. 'She should be in a Home or a nice little bungalow in Fairfield. Come on, I'll take you back there in the car.'

Back at the seemingly lifeless cottage, they were soon through the front door. Betty was lying unconscious on the living room floor, but was clearly breathing. After that, events moved swiftly. Betty did not have a telephone in the cottage, so Kath and Marina stayed with her while Mr Bell bumped and lurched down the track again to his farm where he telephoned for an ambulance. The paramedics managed to drive the ambulance over the first field, but were obliged to tramp over the second field with a stretcher and other equipment.

It was nearly 4am before the two women finally arrived back at their respective homes. Despite their arduous and extraordinary night they were in the office the following day, or rather later the same day, and held the rest of us in thrall with their account of events. Later we heard that Betty had suffered a stroke. Some weeks later she insisted on returning to her cottage.

Our urban counterparts, social workers in the cities, tend to claim that bucolic social work is a soft option. Not so. How many of them are ever likely to tackle such a situation? That

I could think along these lines shows how far I had come since my Sheffield days. I began to perceive that I was myself gradually becoming a country dweller with an essentially rural outlook.

By this time there had been a change of team leader. Geoff had returned to his beloved Yorkshire, and his replacement, Kate, was a very different kettle of fish. Clearly intelligent and efficient, she was also equally clearly a disturbed and deeply unhappy woman. Sometimes she would absent herself for days from the office without notifying anyone as to where she was or the cause of her absence. Once she casually remarked that she frequently vomited, and one or two of us wondered if she were bulimic. Because of this instability we had no real direction or management from the team, and as a result we team members tended to close ranks and support each other. We also, from time to time, indulged in moments of great hilarity which helped to relieve the tension inevitably arising from a stressful job.

Any outsider witnessing these moments would have been horrified, just as I was when, as a young, naive social work student, I looked on with dismay and disapproval as the probation officers mimicked one of their clients. The latter apparently made quite frequent appearances in Court and was fond of a tipple, whipping out a hip flask and taking a quick swig even when being addressed by the Magistrate. Whenever the probation officers felt in need of letting off steam, they would re-enact this courtroom scene within the four walls of the office. Years later, as a fully fledged social worker, I understood completely the need to indulge in this sort of behaviour.

The day after an intruder entered the Queen's bedroom, there was much light-hearted discussion about the incident in the office. Some of us speculated as to why Prince Philip had apparently not been present and seen the unwelcome visitor off the premises with a few well chosen and unrepeatable invectives. Bill concluded that he must have paid a visit to the toilet at that particular point and thereby missed the intruder. We all spent a considerable amount of time that morning suggesting reasons for Prince Philip's absence.

Life in the streets outside the Council offices, as viewed from the windows, also offered entertainment and subject matter for speculation. Opposite the main entrance, on the other side of the street was situated the local vets' surgery. Not only the general public with their pets, but also various vets could be seen coming and going throughout the day. One vet in particular sparked spirited arguments amongst the social work team members, as there was some doubt about this person's gender. Decidedly butch and masculine looking and always dressed in mannish grey trousers and a check shirt, he/she nonetheless sported a definite bust, as I was always at pains to point out. On one occasion Vernon, determined to gain a closer look, threw up the sash window and leaned out dangerously far. Several of us seized his ankles seconds before what would almost certainly have been a fatal plunge to the pavement below.

Let it not be thought that we responsible local authority employees spent all our time immersing ourselves in idle frivolity. Far from it. These little episodes of hilarity were few and far between, and 99 per cent of the time was devoted to our demanding work.

Incidentally, we never did solve the gender puzzle!

Chapter Ten

Work with children was not my scene, I decided, and I felt I no longer wished to be involved with this client group. The unedifying experience with Joanne and Frank and their children brought me to this conclusion. After discussing this dilemma with my team leader, I made the decision to concentrate on the elderly, and people with a mental handicap.

In the 1980s adult training centres, or ATCs as they were usually dubbed, featured prominently in the lives of many mentally handicapped people. The latter could attend these centres after leaving school in order to work in a sheltered environment, learning how to master tasks such as constructing pallets or simple garden furniture, or perhaps Christmas crackers. The aim in theory was for the attenders to move on to a job in the outside world, although in practice many never achieved this.

William was a young boy in his teens when I first met him, the youngest of six children. He had five older sisters, and his parents must have experienced acute distress when their longed for son was born at last, but with mental handicaps. William was actually quite capable in many ways, and it was estimated that he possessed the IQ of a child of ten. He attended the local ATC (Adult Training Centre) and seemed to enjoy this. After a while he became very friendly with another attender, a girl called Jean, and it soon became evident that the relationship had moved beyond the bounds of platonic friendship. Staff at the ATC were not particularly happy about this and, while they did not make overt efforts to keep William and Jean apart, it was clear to me that they privately considered a sexual relationship between two people with a mental handicap was not to be encouraged, and looked askance at me because I was positive about the friendship. Perhaps they considered me to be some kind of wierdo!

It fell to me, as William's social worker, to discover what, if any, sex education William had received at school. His mother, Joan, with whom I had established a good relationship, suggested William and I should meet for a discussion at their house. It transpired that William was not nearly so ignorant of sexual matters as the ATC staff had feared, and had in fact received a good grounding in the basics at his special school.

My view, which was probably slightly in advance of the times, was that the mentally handicapped have as much right to sexual and emotional relationships as anyone else. Now, at the outset of the twenty-first century, this view is generally accepted. William decided that he wished to leave the parental home and move into a flat of his own. Again, I felt that a young person in his late teens had a right to become independent if he so wished, regardless of disability.

I shared many experiences and traumatic life events with this young man and his family. His father died suddenly after I had been working with the family for some months. Not long after this, William developed a mental illness on top of his learning disability which was eventually diagnosed as hebephrenia, a type of schizophrenia which tends to affect young adults. The diagnosis and treatment of this illness involved many a car journey to a nearby hospital with William and Joan to see a consultant psychiatrist.

These sessions lasted an inordinate length of time as the psychiatrist appeared to take a three-hour lunch break. His afternoon outpatients' clinic was supposed to start at 2pm but he never put in an appearance before 3pm – having been absent since midday! No one knew where he went during this time, according to the staff at the reception desk. In the waiting room I looked around at the other bored and despondent patients, all of them suffering from some kind of mental illness, and contemplated writing a letter of complaint to the local paper, but decided against this for fear it might have unfortunate repercussions for the patients.

Once summonsed to the inner sanctum, however, my irritation tended to evaporate, as the psychiatrist was most approachable. William's illness could be kept under control through regular injections, and his behaviour soon became more rational and stable.

William persisted in his wish to live independently. Joan, struggling to come to terms with the loss of her husband, was reluctant to support this idea, and the ATC staff were lukewarm. My relationship with Joan became a little strained. However, a suitable flat was found for William, and a home care assistant was provided on a daily basis, who supervised William's daily living activities such as meal preparation, and made sure that he arrived at the ATC every morning at the correct time.

William was thrilled by his new status and 'bonded' successfully with the home carers, but this situation provoked another hurdle for me to overcome. I became aware after a short while that Joan was jealous of the home care assistants, who were in effect a type of mother substitute. Gradually, after much discussion, she came to accept that William's new way of life represented progress for him, and was in fact proof that she had helped him develop as far as he was able in a very positive way and had not, like so many parents of handicapped children, held him captive in an over-protected cocoon. Now William, like any other young person, had flown the nest and was managing successfully on his own with a little support.

However, Jean's family had a very different attitude. They were reluctant to encourage the friendship and only allowed Jean to see William at the ATC, much to his disappointment. But on the whole he blossomed, and made the best of this situation. Some years later he acquired a part-time job at the leisure centre in Eastbury, travelling there and back independently by bus, thus proving that people with learning difficulties can overcome these difficulties and adopt a similar lifestyle to that of their so-called 'normal' fellow humans.

Not only ATCs but also residential hostels for the mentally handicapped played a prominent part in the lives of some handicapped people who for various reasons were not able to live at home for large chunks of the time. One girl with whom I worked, called Sheila H, lived largely in a hostel and went home to her family for a week or two at a time fairly regularly. During these periods at home I used to visit her and her parents and sometimes brother and sister. The atmosphere was often sticky as one mountain I had to climb took the form of the father's negative attitude towards social workers. According to him, the family had had to struggle entirely on their own for the first few years of Sheila's life without professional support, as no organisation was sufficiently interested to become involved. When eventually a social worker did appear at their home in the West of England, she seemed apathetic and disinclined to intervene actively. Mr H's attitude to the social work profession was strongly coloured by this experience, and his manner towards me was one of cold hostility.

The aim of the Hs was to have Sheila admitted to one of the residential 'villages' for the mentally handicapped, communities where residents lived and worked together in ordinary houses, supported by supervisors and residential social workers who also lived in the community. Sheila's parents clearly expected me to expedite her entry into one of these villages, but places were much sought after and waiting lists were lengthy.

One hot July day I drove Sheila and her mother over to view one of these communities, situated some miles away. En route we stopped for lunch at a roadside pub. Sheila's behaviour was above reproach but nonetheless, because her appearance and conversation were 'different', we drew many curious glances from other occupants of the pub, not all of them benign. For the first time I could perceive with clarity how the families of the handicapped must feel when surrounded by 'normal' people.

Sheila's parents were also anxious that I should see Sheila taking part in ordinary, everyday family activities. Hence the invitation to lunch one day to partake of the family meal while Sheila was present. Mrs H had evidently taken a considerable amount of trouble over providing a tasty casserole, and placed great emphasis on the fact that all her cakes were home baked. However, the atmosphere prevailing in the house was somewhat short of idyllic, as Sheila's teenage sister and brother became involved in heated arguments with each other and with their mother. Flashpoint arrived when the teenage sister wagged an accusing finger at her amply padded mother and announced: 'You're supposed to be on a diet, but who was scoffing a Mars Bar behind the bathroom door this morning!' Mrs H looked as if she were on the verge of collapse or tears, whereupon I felt obliged to intervene hastily with assurances that I was well used to similar scenes in my own home.

Sheila did not, in the end, go to live in one of the village communities. I could never quite make up my mind whether her parents genuinely thought this was the most appropriate setting for her or whether, deep down, they did not really want her as an integral part of their family. Although quite severely handicapped, she possessed a remarkable memory and could unfailingly recall events and people. Every time I appeared on the scene, sometimes long after I had ceased working with the case, whether by chance in the street or in her own home, or at the hostel, she would become quite animated and declare to the world: 'My social worker!' Sheila enjoyed life in the hostel and she continued to live there indefinitely, returning to the family home at intervals.

Although the bulk of my caseload centred on the elderly and those with a mental handicap, we were all obliged to take on a small number of miscellaneous cases. I was, for example, asked to visit a man in his 30s, living alone and in receipt of a small amount of supplementary benefit, now known as income support. His GP expressed concern about his ability to support himself and wondered if the Social Services could advise on the provision of clothes.

This lone gentleman resided in a small village some ten miles from Fairfield. As there was no reply to my knock, I walked in as is customary in rural areas. In the middle of a cluttered living room, with the curtains drawn (it was early afternoon) stood a man of medium height. There was nothing remarkable about him apart from the fact that he was wearing dark glasses, and had an unnerving habit of seemingly staring intently without speaking.

'Hello, Mr F, Dr Peterson asked me to visit to see if we could do anything to help,' I explained, feeling somewhat disconcerted by the man's silent demeanour.

Suddenly he jerked into movement and speech, like a wound-up clockwork toy. 'Call me Basil. I like to be informal. Come nearer and sit on this chair.'

Perching myself awkwardly on the edge of the chair he indicated, I realised, too late, that I had failed to follow the golden rule that all social workers should heed: 'Keep yourself between the client and the door.' This strange man was standing between me and the door, much to my discomfiture.

Somewhat hastily, I explained that I could arrange for him to have some clothes from the WRVS clothing store, if he so wished. Mr F (I stuck resolutely to the more formal surname) said he did wish, and in return he would give me some clothes which had belonged to his late mother and which could be passed on to some needy elderly. Whereupon he rummaged in the depths of a large cupboard and brought forth two enormous plastic carriers. These he placed on the floor by my chair, dipped his hand into one of them and produced what appeared to be some kind of blouse. Once upon a time it had probably been white, but was now an indeterminate shade of grey. A strong, fusty odour emanated from the bags and I made a mental note to consign them to the nearest litter bin – provided, that is, I ever managed to escape from the house!

Mr F pushed the blouse back into the bag, and straightened up again. With slow, deliberate movements, he removed the dark glasses to reveal one pale blue eye and what appeared to be an empty socket. He gazed at me intently, his one eye moving slowly from my neck down to my legs. It was a warm day in mid-summer, and I was wearing a short-sleeved cotton dress, no tights and flimsy sandals. I found myself fervently wishing that a large, shapeless cloak would suddenly materialise and wrap itself loosely round me so that this bizarre male would have nothing to stare at.

'Wouldn't you like to sit down, Mr F, and then we could have a talk.' I had arrived at this house as a social worker, so a social worker I had better try to be.

'No,' replied Mr F, 'I prefer standing. If you're going to get some clothes for me, you'll need to know my measurements, won't you.' He placed his hand on the back of my chair and bent down until his face was virtually touching mine. 'You can start by measuring my inside leg.' His voice was by now a suggestive whisper. 'I have a tape measure on the table over there.'

I decided to abandon the role of social worker, slid off the edge of the chair and managed to shuffle across the room to the door leading out into the road. Yanking the handle down,

I whipped open the door, breathed goodbye over my shoulder and fled to my car.

Once back in the safety of the office, I marched straight in to see the team leader. 'If another home visit is required to this client, you'll have to send a male social worker,' I declared, after relating my unnerving experience. She agreed that this would be appropriate, but I nonetheless received a berating for allowing the interview to get out of hand.

—o0o—

In the early 1980s the role of home help began to change and evolve. For several decades prior to that, home helps had assisted sick or handicapped people of all age groups with practical tasks such as housework and shopping. Now this role expanded to include help with personal care tasks like washing and bathing. Social workers carried out the assessments, that is, they attempted to ascertain as accurately as possible what the clients' needs were; then this assessment was passed on to a home care officer whose job it was to organise the home care input.

Working as I did with many elderly people, I became much involved with the home care scene. At one stage during the mid 80s I started wearing two hats, which at that time was unique within -----shire Social Services Department. Kath, the home care officer, embarked on a three-year social work training course which she undertook while continuing with her job. Because the course entailed periods of college attendance and study leave, another person was needed to help out with the organisation of home care. Into the breach I stepped, acting as social worker for part of each week and as a home care officer for the rest of the time. This novel experience, and particularly the whole new world of organising home care packages and managing groups of home care assistants (as home helps were now called), was to stand me in good stead in later years after I had left Fairfield, although I did not know this at the time.

The Fairfield office covered a large chunk of -----shire, which contained a significant percentage of elderly inhabitants. I found myself travelling a considerable number of miles when arranging home care packages or carrying out reviews. I was soon to discover that a goodly sprinkling of frail, dependent older people living in this area were not natives of -----shire but had decided to retire here, mainly because they had spent enjoyable holidays in the area.

Many of these were highly educated, intelligent people who had held down good jobs during their working lives, but whose informed minds, astonishingly, seemed to grow blinkers at the point of retirement. An active and healthy 65-year-old may be a very different person 15 or 20 years hence, and maybe much sooner, possibly needing to rely heavily on local services, and in many cases situated hundreds of miles from their roots, families and friends. Quite frequently I came across these blinkered clients who had clearly never really considered all the possible aspects of retirement and old age, some of them living in isolated spots far from all amenities.

Part of a welfare assistant's remit consisted of a restricted number of 'easier' cases, although quite frequently some of these turned out to be astonishingly complex. My colleague, Val, who worked as the welfare assistant in the Fairfield office, was becoming increasingly worried about one such case she had visited in a sparsely populated valley, an elderly couple who were struggling to cope with their everyday lives but who were reluctant to accept home care or any other service. Val had warned me about the remoteness of their house, but just how remote I was yet to find out. I agreed to visit this couple, together with Val, to see if we could prevail upon them to change their minds.

We had agreed to meet at one of the residential homes in the local small town, and set off from there. Because I knew that we would have to undertake part of the trek on foot, I had come suitably clad in trousers and anorak, with my wellies stashed away in the car boot. However, Val was somewhat puzzlingly dressed in an expensive-looking trench coat and court shoes and wielding a smart black umbrella, which would have looked more in place on a London pavement than this rural outback. It was early December, cold and gloomy, and the customary -----shire weather of high winds and horizontal rain prevailed.

I drove as far as I could, following Val's directions. We were then obliged to leave the car parked on the road and set off across a squelching field. My wellies coped manfully with this, but Val's city shoes protested and began to sink beneath the oozing mud. What was that moving, glinting ribbon at the far end of this long, sloping meadow? As we drew nearer, I realised with a sense of dismay that it was a fair-sized, fast-flowing brook, swollen beyond its normal size by the recent persistent rain.

I stopped in my tracks and turned to Val. 'You didn't tell me about a stream,' I said rather reproachfully. 'We'll have to find another way round it.'

Val pulled her right foot out of the sodden earth with a sucking noise. 'There isn't another way,' she pronounced matter-of-factly. 'The only way is across the beck.'

Easier said than done, especially when you were wearing court shoes. Even my wellies might not cope with this swollen waterway. After much tramping up and down the muddy bank, I came across a row of large stones which had been placed rather haphazardly across the brook, clearly intended as a makeshift crossing place. Having tried in vain to persuade Val to return to the car while I forged on alone to the house, we gingerly embarked on our watery journey to the opposite bank, Val by this time having abandoned all pretence at keeping her shoes clean and dry.

The stones were slippery and not firmly anchored to the bed of the stream. Consequently, before we were even halfway across, we had both slipped off the stones and were plunging about wildly, up to our knees in painfully cold, rushing water. Somehow we made it to the far bank, crossed two more fields, climbed over a gate, and stumbled down a steep path leading to a large stone-built house. Just before we reached the back door, I stopped in my tracks once more and surveyed us both. We bore a closer resemblance to a couple of water rats than human beings representing a large public organisation about to call on a couple of needy clients. Val took off her shoes, now reduced to two pathetic pieces of shapeless, sodden leather, and looked sadly at the remains of her tights. 'Oh well, at least my umbrella came in useful,' she said, determined to remain positive. It had indeed. When I finally reached the far bank of the beck I had grasped the rolled up umbrella, which Val was still clutching, and used it to pull her out of the water and on to the slippery bank.

I took off my dripping anorak, which had once been blue but was now streaked with murky brown splashes of mud, and raised my hand to the doorbell. 'Now,' I said, 'we'll have to set about convincing these people that we are neither bizarre aquatic creatures nor wandering vagrants, but respectable county council workers.'

In fact Mr and Mrs W accepted our explanation of our untoward appearance and, following a lengthy talk, also accepted our suggestions concerning home care. As we were speaking, I started wondering how on earth the home care assistants were going to manage the difficult trek to this house, but did not voice my misgivings. We'll cross that bridge when we come to it, I decided, or rather, that wobbly line of stepping stones.

This frail couple had originated from the Midlands and, like too many others, had fulfilled their dream of spending their twilight years in -----shire. They did not seem to have given much consideration to the fact that the house they had chosen was not only ten miles from the nearest shop and two miles from the nearest neighbours, but also virtually inaccessible from the road. Mrs W, aged 85, had reached a fairly advanced stage of dementia, while her 90-year-old husband, bowed and gnarled with arthritis, tried desperately to cope with her, look after himself and run the house. The result was two pathetic, undernourished, shabby old people living in a chaotic house with bundles of unwashed clothes stashed in corners, and a kitchen where mice ran merrily over cluttered work surfaces.

A similar case concerned Mrs Y, an elderly woman living alone in a house that she and her husband had designed and built when they retired. It was situated in part of a field which the couple had bought from a local farmer. This house was just about the ugliest edifice I have ever had the misfortune to set eyes on, and how planning permission had ever been granted was cause for conjecture. Perhaps Mr and Mrs Y had influential connections in the planning department!

Geographical and social isolation was again a striking feature in this case. The couple were not indigenous and had lived and worked in Northampton prior to their retirement. Within two years of his 65th birthday, Mr Y was dead, struck down, like so many others, by a massive heart attack, and a few years later his widow fell prey to a serious illness. The house they had built was situated three miles from the nearest village, about seven or eight miles west of Fairfield. Mrs Y's only relative was a sister, also in poor health and living 500 miles away in Somerset.

The Social Services, as so often happens, were called upon to help when the situation had reached crisis point. Mrs Y could no longer drive because of her health problems, and was consequently stranded in her unappealing house in the middle of the field, unable to shop, go to the bank or visit the doctor.

The first time I visited I drove to the house along a maze of winding lanes, hedges and trees verdant with May foliage. This was the rural idyll that lured so many people, the utopian vision of bucolic bliss that drove otherwise rational people at the end of their working lives to buy or build homes in unsuitably remote locations.

As the house came into view and its unappetising facade caused a sharp intake of breath and a muttered 'Oh, no!', I became aware of a lively object running and jumping about in the unkempt garden. A dog. A large dog. An Alsatian. I have always been an animal lover, but Alsatians are placed at the top of my mental list of least favourite dogs as a result of a traumatic childhood experience when an eight-year-old friend was mauled by one of these dogs in a totally unprovoked incident.

The car came to a halt outside the front gate. The dog stood on its hind legs and pushed its front paws against the gate, ear-shattering barks drowning out the sound of the car engine which I had not yet switched off. My job quite frequently included encounters with animals, most of these amicable and welcome encounters, but with one or two notable exceptions.

This dithering outside a front gate reminded me vividly of the time I had driven out to visit an elderly woman whose home was an isolated cottage high on a hillside. My long-suffering car had groaned its way up a steep fellside lane and jolted to a halt outside the house. My eye immediately fell upon a large handwritten notice stuck to the gatepost, which announced in bold lettering: 'Beware of cock! Take stick.' A collection of sticks of varying lengths and thicknesses lay on the grass by the gate. I scrambled out of the car and stood, irresolute, by the pile of sticks, wondering if I should, on encountering a fierce cock, merely brandish a stick in a meaningful manner or actually hit the bird with it, which I was certainly loath to contemplate. However, I was rescued from this dilemma by a figure waving from an upstairs window. 'Are you the welfare lady? It's all right, lass. Cock's shut up in the bothy.'

Now, as I switched off the engine and emerged from the car, it looked as if I was again going to be spared an alarming encounter with an aggressive animal. A hunched up person was standing in the porch calling to the dog, which obediently stopped hurling itself against the gate, trotted down the path to the front door and disappeared into the gloom within.

'You can come in. Rambo's gone into the kitchen,' called a wavering voice.

This preliminary interview with the lady passed off reasonably well, although I was uncomfortably aware of Rambo's intermittent barks and rattling noises coming from the kitchen door. It was clear from my conversation with the elderly client that Rambo was a much treasured companion, that she had no real friends in the area, and that she now regretted retiring to a part of the country where she had no roots. She was suffering from Paget's disease and felt that she might not have much longer to live. About impending death she showed little dread; her all-consuming anxiety was focussed on Rambo's possible fate after she had gone. He was well known to the staff of a nearly kennels where he had been boarded out at intervals when Mr and Mrs Y were away, and latterly when his mistress was obliged to spend time in hospital. I made a mental note to contact them to discuss contingency plans.

Fortunately I was able to arrange daily home care for Mrs Y. While taking down her financial details I noted with surprise that she was in receipt of supplementary benefit. How had the Ys come to such a pass? Both had been professional people with good salaries. How and why had they come to the end of their financial resources? This was a question that was never answered as Mrs Y chose not to disclose the background to her financial situation.

My second visit took place again in the living room, with Rambo this time shut outside in the garden, where he raced up and down the lawn in a frenzied fashion, barking frantically. On leaving, I made an unceremonious dash from the front door to the gate, preceded by a large gambolling dog. Would he let me through the gate? To my horror, the latch appeared to be jammed. Throwing caution to the winds, I decided to throw my case and handbag over the gate, after which I climbed, in a highly undignified fashion, over the garden wall, much to the entertainment of the farm worker repairing a hedge on the opposite side of the road. How I ever accomplished this feat I shall never know, as I was wearing a tight, straight skirt that morning. To be fair to Rambo, although he made a lot of noise and was particularly fond of bounding quite high in the air, he did not have an aggressive manner and seemed quite disappointed to see me go.

When I arrived at the house on the third occasion, Rambo was in the living room with Mrs Y. She was lying on the sofa and it was clearly one of her bad days. She apologised for not getting up and remarked that Rambo would have to stay in the room with us, but she was sure he would be good. Rambo's idea of good behaviour was to run around the room, periodically crashing into occasional tables and sending knick knacks flying with flailing paws and tail.

I offered to make Mrs Y a cup of tea. On returning from the kitchen with two cups, I managed to set them down on top of the TV set without mishap, and then turned round with the aim of sitting down in a nearby chair. Before I could do this, however, Rambo had bounded across the room, raised himself on his hind legs and pinned me against the wall with his front paws clamped on my shoulders. To say I was petrified would be an understatement. Rambo was completely deaf to his mistress's entreaties to come to her and leave me alone. Perhaps he considered this to be some kind of game, for he did not snarl and made no attempt to bite me. Trying to hide my fear, and by this time feeling decidedly foolish, I had no choice but to stay flattened against the wall and conduct the interview in this position, like a trapped butterfly on display. After about ten minutes Rambo lost interest in this 'game', dropped his paws and trotted off to the far end of the room to inspect a nest of tables he had overturned earlier. I managed to execute a speedy exit.

Soon after this Mrs Y was admitted to hospital, which was to be her last resting place. Rambo had been collected by one of the kennel staff shortly before the ambulance arrived. Two weeks later, Mrs Y died and I wondered what would happen to Rambo. I had visited her in hospital where she had spoken movingly of her attachment to this large, exuberant dog. When I telephoned the kennels and spoke to the owner, she said she was certain she could find a good home for Rambo and in fact already had someone suitable in mind. It transpired that Mrs Y had never paid the required weekly charge for Rambo's keep, but had merely contributed what she could afford. The kennels owner had accepted this without demur, knowing that Mrs Y was living in decidedly reduced circumstances.

Since this 'canine experience', although still fearful when encountering an Alsatian, I now know that this breed of dog is not always a leaping bundle of bad intentions and deadly fangs.

Not all my elderly clients, needless to say, were 'incomers' like the Ws and Mrs Y. The bulk, in fact, were indigenous inhabitants living in villages and small towns where they had always lived with relatives nearby. A considerable number of family relationships were anything but harmonious, and my colleagues and I encountered many inter-generational conflicts. In other cases, even when the elderly people were surrounded by genuinely helpful sons and daughters, nothing could alleviate the sadness and feelings of doom-laden hopelessness, so often companions of old age.

One such client was Tommy, whose dwelling place for many decades had been an old terraced house on the edge of Fairfield. Here he lived with his beloved cat, which by the time I arrived on the scene had attained the distinguished age of 18. Entering Tommy's home was akin to stepping into a time warp. Nothing appeared to have been changed since the early years of the century, including the lighting arrangements. Electricity had never been installed and instead there were flaring, hissing gas brackets in each room.

Tommy's daughter lived in another part of Fairfield, about 15 minutes' walk away. She was becoming increasingly worried about her father, who had lost interest in everything except his cat, and did not wish to eat. In his prime Tommy had been an active member of the community and had worked as a labourer on the roads for many years. Now in his 80s, he felt useless, superfluous and on the scrap heap. 'When the bin men come to empty my bin, I feel they should take me away as well,' he confided to me. My suggestions as to how this situation might be alleviated along the lines of day care attendance or coach trips with the over 60s fell on stony ground. Tommy simply did not wish to cross the threshold into the outside world. He did agree to a daily visit from a home care assistant whose main task, apart from some housework and ironing, was to prepare a meal for him and encourage him to eat it.

Things seemed to be looking up a little, and Tommy began to respond to the home carer's friendly overtures and tasty offerings, when disaster struck. Tigger, the cat, died quietly in the middle of the night on his old blanket draped over the ancient settee, one of the flaring gas lights keeping watch over him on the wall above.

From this moment on, Tommy went downhill. He saw no reason to carry on living, and felt death would be infinitely preferable to the futility of his present existence. A few months after Tigger's demise, Tommy followed his departed companion into the next world. He had clearly made a conscious decision to die.

Chapter Eleven

'All human beings are resistant to change – some are more resistant than others.'

Years before, in what now seemed like another era in another world, Eric Sainsbury, the senior lecturer in charge of my social work training course, had made this pronouncement. Nothing particularly profound or original, but it had lingered in the recesses of my brain.

By the end of the 1980s change was in the air, and I felt the time was ripe for me to change, too, and make a move away from Fairfield, although part of me strongly resisted this. Management consultants were a fashionable breed during this decade, and -----shire County Council had decided to jump on the bandwagon and employ one of these firms, at vast expense, to examine the workings of the Social Services department and several other departments, and to make recommendations. The consultants came to the conclusion that the Social Services were in need of a fairly radical makeover. One of the changes recommended, and the one which was to have the most far-reaching effect on the front-line workers, was a switch from generic to specialist teams.

Most of us had never worked within a specialist team, although two areas in -----shire had been operating pilot specialist schemes for the past six or seven years. The new director of Social Services, an intellectual visionary, devised a new framework and fleshed out the bones with details of how he wanted his dream to work. I and my colleagues at Fairfield were jolted out of our busy but safe and familiar world which had trundled along, virtually unchanged, for ten years or more, and had to face up to the fact that the end of an era was nigh. First and foremost, we each had to decide which specialist team to join. I also had to prod myself into deciding whether to apply for jobs in other districts. Some of my favourite colleagues were drifting away, one by one, to other parts of -----shire, or even other parts of Britain in order to establish themselves in different jobs and different teams before the new structure was launched.

The level of anxiety amongst us all was very high as we faced the approaching, quite fundamental, reorganisation. Over the years I have sometimes wondered whether those in high places who decide upon and draw up radical departmental changes ever really consider the toll this takes on staff in the field, their immediate line managers, and the administrative support staff. Some people welcome the challenge and stimulation of change and a step into the unknown, but they are probably a minority; most fear change and find it difficult to deal with the resulting feelings of stress.

A suitable job with Eastbury Social Services was advertised and I took the plunge and applied for it. Interviews terrify me and every intelligent thought vacates my brain, so I was genuinely surprised when I was offered this job. The launch of the revamped department was still three to four months away, and I would be joining briefly a team called Older People's Team which had been in operation for approximately the past seven years. I would only just be getting to grips with this new experience when the old order would cease and I, together with my new colleagues, would be obliged to enter the brave new world. But more about this later.

Because of my experience of working with the elderly, people with learning difficulties and, to a certain extent, the younger physically handicapped, I could choose from these three client groups which specialist team to join. This proved to be quite a dilemma. However, after I had accepted the job in Eastbury, I knew that I would be specialising in work with the elderly and that there was no going back.

Leaving Fairfield was a wrench, but I knew that following reorganisation the set-up there would be very different from the old generic team structure, with few of my old colleagues remaining. As I left the office for the last time at Christmas 1988 and prepared to face a new job in a strange office with strange colleagues in the New Year, it occurred to me that all this turmoil, change and shaking up resembled the kaleidoscope my grandmother had given me as a child. You squinted down the tube and saw an intricate pattern, each tiny piece with its own specific place in the pattern. Then you shook the tube and looked again and beheld a completely different pattern. We employees of the Social Services department were being shaken out of one pattern and being made to form another willy nilly, with little control over the process.

This upheaval in my working life took place against an equally tempestuous domestic backdrop. The usual adolescent traumas and conflicts had been compounded by the unwelcome drama being enacted within my daughter's school, one of the nine Quaker schools in England. For two years it had been failing and disintegrating due to severe financial problems, and finally closed down immediately after she sat her 'O' Levels.

In addition to this turbulent scenario I had to live through a series of seemingly never-ending crises connected with my husband's firm, a small family civil engineering business. Towards the end of the Thatcher years, the construction industry began to crumple, and before long was on its knees. My home life could scarcely be described as equable.

And equable I certainly did not feel as I joined the Older People's Team in the town hall in Eastbury. The many differences between my new office and the old one in Fairfield were so stark that I could scarcely believe that I was not in a completely different county, let alone that I was still working for the same department just 11 miles down the road!

Where was the climate of professionalism? Where had all the men gone? Why were there so many women here? Why was I looked at askance as if I were some bizarre breed just landed from Mars when I asked to see copies of our in-house journals 'Social Work Today' and 'Community Care'? No one reads those here, I was informed. At Fairfield there had been at least half a dozen of us who, during moments of relaxation over mugs of coffee, had held animated discussions on such topics as the TV dramatisation of 'Brideshead Revisited'. Had anyone here even heard of Evelyn Waugh? The only interest apparent here seemed to be enthusiastic attendance at Union meetings. At the Fairfield office we had all been nominal members of NALGO, but going to a Union meeting came very low on most people's lists of things to do. We had on the whole been middle-of-the-road 'Guardian' readers with no leanings towards extreme views, and instinctive feelings of distaste at the prospect of striking social workers.

However, a display of intellectual and professional snobbery was hardly likely to stand me in good stead, and I told myself firmly that working amongst a group of people of a different ilk was what I needed. I therefore buckled down to a few short months' hard work with the Older People's team.

For a long time it seemed strange to be working with the elderly only and to be surrounded by colleagues who could only discuss this client group. I had been used to exchanging stimulating ideas with social workers who were working with child abuse cases or dealing with complex mental health issues as well as concentrating on my own particular kind of case.

Now I seemed to be moving through a narrow tunnel, cut off from a wider perspective of the social work scene.

The work itself, the assessment of the needs of elderly clients, I was familiar with but the new territory, mainly within Eastbury, seemed strange, dreary and depressing. It was the depths of winter when I embarked on this new job, a grey cheerless season which did not render the endless trips to faceless, dilapidated housing estates exactly uplifting. I began to wonder if the rest of my working life would consist of this pattern and thought wistfully of the variety of locations I had been used to when based at Fairfield, mainly rural or semi-rural. Again, it dawned on me that I had moved a long way from my days of urban dwelling in Sheffield when the stuff of my daily existence consisted of visiting clients imprisoned in high rise flats or searching for an address amongst row upon row of terraced houses. Now I was yearning for remote hamlets and isolated cottages!

Time moved on very swiftly and the dreaded 'D day' was almost upon us. The 'patch-centred' system was a concept dreamed up by our seniors and betters. Those of us who would be forming the new teams would be dealing mainly with the frail elderly, but because we would each be in charge of a group of home care assistants who would work not only for the elderly but for all other client groups as well, we were clearly going to have a less narrow remit than if we had been confined to the elderly only. This I welcomed, and I was profoundly thankful that I had at least had some experience of managing home carers. Most of my colleagues, for whom this was a totally novel venture, were wracked with apprehension. The tense and fearful atmosphere was almost palpable.

Each social worker would be operating within a 'patch' in Eastbury and its environs , which consists of outlying country areas as well as the city of Eastbury itself. The manager of the Older People's Team (by the end of the 80s 'manager' had become a ubiquitous buzz word), who would also become the manager of one of the brand new teams, selected a patch for each team member. I was informed that my patch was to be the Ashton area. Ashton is a small town surrounded by a large expanse of remote, empty, and hauntingly beautiful countryside.

During my first couple of weeks' employment with Eastbury Social Services I had spent time visiting all the residential homes for the elderly in the district, which included brief forays into the Ashton area, but it was still virtually unknown to me. I felt some relief at knowing that I was not to be confined to one of the less salubrious parts of Eastbury, and mildly curious about my new territory, but at that stage I had no inkling of how important it was to become to me.

Our work was a combination of assessment of need, organising and putting into operation tailor-made care packages, and overseeing the work of the home care assistants in the patch. Each group of home carers possessed a sort of foreman, or rather woman, known as a patch carer, whose principal task was to draw up weekly work rotas while working as a home carer herself at the same time. The first time I met the Ashton patch carer there was an immediate rapport between us, and I felt confident we were going to work well together. At our first meeting I was eyed curiously by the assembled women, about ten in all, who probably wondered how this stranger from the town hall would shape up in this outpost of the Ashton region. About two thirds of these women lived and worked in Ashton itself; the rest were from the remote rural area outside Ashton, stretching up to the next county border.

In the following months and years I was to become well acquainted with this as yet little known corner of -----shire. Here was something different, something apart, unspoilt, almost unpopulated.

As I drove around on my way to visit clients in far-flung places, I became acutely aware of the almost tangible atmosphere of peace. But that was all in the future. At the initial meeting with the home care staff, I tried to digest details of clients in the patch in addition to other information such as the number of residential homes, day centres, etc, and realised that the job ahead of me was yet another step into the unknown.

Chapter Twelve

The bulk of my time was spent in the patch. Obviously I had to be in the office at least part of every day in order to use the telephone and forge my way through sheaves of paperwork. Another anxiety-provoking bogey was beginning to raise its head in the form of Information Technology but at this stage I chose to ignore the computer terminals appearing in every office and strove doggedly on with files, biro and paper.

Each time my car left the outskirts of Eastbury and swung out onto the busy A road in the direction of Ashton, I heaved a sigh of relief. I quickly felt at home here and within a surprisingly short time had become acquainted with all the key people and organisations in the area. One of the best features of the patch system was the opportunity afforded to each social worker to initiate new projects in his or her own patch. Together with local WRVS workers I helped to set up a new day centre for the elderly, particularly for those living in isolated locations, and my very own brainchild was the launch of monthly get-togethers with local people who were in any way connected with the elderly or other vulnerable groups or individuals. These gatherings included not only district nurses, housing officials, and staff from the residential homes but also such figures as the headmaster of the local comprehensive and the vicar of the parish church. These meetings were very popular and well attended.

Initiatives such as these did not spring up overnight, of course; they took a year or two to develop and begin to flourish. The everyday 'bread and butter' work consisted of visiting new and existing clients, assessing their needs, providing them with services, supervising the home care assistants, both individually and in the form of group supervision – a monthly patch meeting was held at which we discussed cases, particularly those which might be difficult and complex. Sometimes I asked guest speakers to come and give talks on subjects particularly relevant to home carers, such as Parkinson's Disease, visual impairment, or the management of incontinence. On one occasion I invited a speaker from the Institute of Advanced Motorists. Home care assistants working in rural areas have to drive from house to house along almost deserted roads in every type of weather imaginable, and need to be in possession of good driving skills.

I have to confess to a few feelings of apprehension on first learning that each social worker would be line manager to a group of home care assistants, as I did not think this would be my forte. However, I came to find this aspect of the work especially interesting and rewarding. The value of the home care service should never be underestimated; Britain would fall flat on its face should this unsung army of women (and a few men) suddenly vanish. I made a point of meeting each home carer individually on a regular basis, including the patch carer, Christine, to discuss their work and any problems they might have, even personal ones. Christine and I tackled a multitude of problems together and lived through many a sticky moment, but we also indulged in many a laugh! The vital ingredient in social work is a sense of humour. Without that you are certainly at risk of sliding down the slippery slope towards a nervous breakdown.

Some home carers supported individuals or families who did not come within the 'elderly' bracket. This type of case

I liked as it meant I could keep in touch with other client groups. However, some of these cases threw up seemingly insurmountable problems which on occasion could even be frightening and sinister.

One such case consisted of a couple who ran a pub in an extremely remote and startlingly beautiful spot a mile or two from the next county border, and their five children. One of these, a girl aged ten, had quite severe learning difficulties, as mental handicaps were now called, and my predecessor, the by then defunct home care officer (the position, not the person!) had organised home care support in order to give the parents some relief. The home carer visited several times weekly and took total charge of the child so that the mother was able to pay attention to the other children or just relax.

This arrangement had been in operation for some time, but it was not until I started to investigate the case that alarming elements came to light. The home care assistant had come to know the family well and began to voice her concerns to me. It appeared that the father was a violent and unstable man who had perpetrated many acts of physical violence against his wife over a period of more than 15 years, and was now abusing some of the children in the same way, although he never touched the ten-year-old daughter. The home carer based her assertions on her own observations while in the house and on what the girl's mother told her.

This was a delicate situation. My remit was to monitor the home care provision, which was working well. The child with learning difficulties was being well cared for, and there was nothing definite that I could put my finger on or criticise with any assurance, because as yet there was no real evidence of evil or criminal behaviour. However, I was acutely aware that social workers have a duty to investigate the possibility of abuse against children. I have also always felt strongly about domestic violence between husband and wife.

I visited this remote dwelling several times with the aim of talking to the couple and trying to ascertain myself what was going on within the family. I had learnt through the bush telegraph which operates in isolated country areas that the house was full of an assortment of large knives and guns which Keith, the father, had apparently collected over the years. What, I wondered, did the pub regulars think of their strange landlord? Or perhaps he did not behave in a strange or aggressive manner while serving behind the bar.

While I was in their house I did not feel at ease. I had the impression that Keith was watchful and on his guard. He would stand at one end of the kitchen, leaning against the kitchen table, saying little but watching me unsmilingly. Ellen, his wife, was more forthcoming, but would talk about inconsequential matters such as what she proposed to cook for supper that night. Superficially, at least, she did not give the impression of a person enduring continual violence, and I saw no signs of injury or bruising. However, Polly, the home care assistant, maintained that Keith was always careful to hit his wife on parts of the body that were likely to be covered up by clothes. I was always relieved to leave the house.

Polly went on leave for a fortnight and another home carer who stood in for her reported to me that Keith left weapons of one sort or another lying around in the house, including a 'bloody great meat cleaver' across the kitchen table. The home carer felt alarmed at being surrounded by these dangerous objects and concerned because the parents did not appear to perceive the risks to the children.

The crisis came one evening. I had arrived home after a day's work and we had just finished supper when the telephone rang shrilly. It was Polly, the family's regular home carer, now returned from holiday, telephoning from the isolated pub.

I glanced at my watch – 7pm. 'What on earth are you still doing at that place? You should have left two hours ago.'

Polly's voice came floating down the line, quite clear, but high pitched with tension and fear. 'Keith went berserk after he had an argument with Ellen, and he's run off into the woods with one of them big knives and I think he's got a gun with him as well.'

While I tried to digest this frightening information, a vision flashed into my mind's eye of the extensive and dense woodland in the vicinity of the house. It was late September and already nearly dark. What was in Keith's mind? What was he going to do with the knife and the gun?

The line crackled. 'Are you still there?'

Polly's fear-laden, slightly trembling voice reminded me that I had to act sharply and make decisions. 'I daren't leave the pub and go home because Keith might be lurking nearby, and besides, I can't leave Ellen and the children alone. Ellen's serving behind the bar as usual and she's told the customers – there's only two in at the moment – that Keith has gone out for the evening. She and the kids are terrified.'

My mind started moving into fifth gear. 'Try and keep calm, Polly,' I urged rather uselessly. 'I'll 'phone the police straightaway, and various other people. I'll get somebody to you as fast as possible.'

The next half hour whizzed by like a speeded up film. I informed the police and my team manager (fortunately I had his home telephone number in my diary), and he contacted the out-of-hours emergency social work team plus the manager of one of the child protection teams. I was beside myself with anxiety about all concerned in this momentous drama and potential tragedy – about Polly, for whom I felt responsible, about Ellen and about the children.

All the evening I hovered by the telephone. Eventually my team manager rang back to inform me that several police officers, some armed, had searched the woods and eventually cornered Keith, who was indeed in possession of a knife and a gun and declaring that he wished to murder his wife and kids.

The upshot of this frightening incident was that Ellen and the children were escorted by the police to a women's refuge in Eastbury, where they stayed for a couple of weeks. They then all travelled to the South East to live with relatives.

A case conference was held at the town hall to try and address the issue of the alleged physical abuse of two of the children. Ellen attended this conference, and also Polly, which was a considerable ordeal for this quiet countrywoman, especially when she was asked to give an account of what she had observed and been told while working as a home care assistant with the handicapped girl.

The lid was prised off a can of worms. A harsh and sordid picture emerged of many years of brutality, first towards Ellen only, then towards two of the children, a boy and a girl, whom Keith particularly disliked. The boy, the oldest of the five children, had, by the time he reached 16 and grown into a strapping youth, started to retaliate with the aim of defending both himself and his mother and sister. It was depressingly easy to perceive that this lad, whose male role model was an abusing father, would probably form part of the next generation of violent parents.

Later Keith appeared in court but, unbelievably, no charges were brought against him because, it was maintained, of lack of evidence. He returned to the pub and soon acquired a girlfriend who lived and worked in the pub with him. Was he treating her in the same way that he had treated Ellen? (She, as far as I know, has never returned to -----shire.)

Every time I drive around in that little known corner of the county, I marvel at the beauty of the narrow, tree-lined roads, some winding themselves into hairpins, the trees sometimes forming arches above, the classically English green hillocky fields mixed with austerely grandiose stretches of mauve and brown moorland, and the sudden panoramic vistas glimpsed over a hedge. The contrast between the loveliness outside and the ugly violence that was perpetrated within the four walls of an isolated building can scarcely be credited.

Somewhat fancifully, I could not help but wonder if there was some connection with the brutal and bloody history of that area, as those green rolling swards and the depths of the abundant woodlands, centuries ago, had been a constant battleground.

—o0o—

Home care assistants also give vital help to people of all age groups with chronic degenerative diseases. In the centre of Ashton lived a woman in her 50s with motor neurone disease. She had a young son, aged 14, and for a time a husband, but the couple parted company while I was the social worker involved with the case. That is, I was the social worker who monitored the home care input, and because the client was a younger adult, she also had a social worker attached to the team for the younger physically disabled. This social worker and I came to disagree quite fundamentally on how the case was to be handled.

Hannah, the client, was a stirrer and a mischief-maker. Those who had known her since she was a young girl before she had contracted the illness, including one of the district nurses, maintained she was ever thus. By the time I arrived on the scene, the disease had progressed to the point where she needed assistance with every aspect of intimate personal care. Two home carers together would visit several times every day to get Hannah up, washed and dressed, and help with toileting. A close relationship inevitably developed between carers and client. Hannah was by nature outgoing and, as a young girl, had been quite a wild partygoer before her illness struck. She was also earthy and brazen to the point of vulgarity and liked to exchange suggestive jokes with Zoe, one of the home care assistants who was also a down-to-earth person.

One morning, out of the blue, Christine, the patch carer, came to see me while I was sitting in the warden's office within the sheltered housing unit making telephone calls and catching up on paperwork, to say that Hannah had accused Zoe of making sexual advances to her. What's more, according to Christine, this allegation was being taken very seriously by Greg, Hannah's social worker.

My reaction to this disturbing news was one of anger. Hannah was to be pitied, certainly, because of this terrible illness which had struck her down in middle age, but I had observed her devious and manipulative personality and strongly suspected that she was determined to cause trouble. The allegation would have to be investigated, however. I had come to know Zoe quite well and did not think she had any sexual tendencies or intentions of this nature at all.

Greg was very much into the latest theories and ideas about illness, both physical and psychiatric. He maintained that vulnerable people like Hannah were sometimes taken advantage of sexually by those who cared for them and that he knew, from all his reading on such subjects, that motor neurone sufferers were all prone to depression which rendered them even more vulnerable. I harboured grave doubts about the value of lumping all motor neurone victims together in one category. They are, after all, all individuals with different personalities and life experiences, and an illness does not take away that unique personality. Over the years I had worked with several motor neurone sufferers and also had a personal friend with the disease. Each of these people had reacted differently to the various stages of the illness. Depression, understandably, certainly played a part, but by no stretch of the imagination could it be said that these sufferers had suddenly turned into identical jellies in identical moulds.

Because Hannah maintained that several other people in Ashton, also clients, were accusing Zoe of unwelcome sexual attention, I – together with one of the senior social workers – was obliged to move around Ashton interviewing these alleged victims. It quickly became clear that most had no idea what we were talking about; the rest seemed genuinely bewildered by the thought that Zoe, who had lived all her life in Ashton, could be accused of any kind of misdemeanour. We ended up with not one shred of evidence to support Hannah's claim. After speaking to each of the other two home care assistants who regularly accompanied Zoe into Hannah's house, I came to the conclusion that Hannah, probably out of boredom and feelings of resentment against her enforced inactivity, had determined to bring some excitement into her life by becoming chief mischief-maker in this small community.

Zoe herself was visibly upset by these accusations and vehemently denied any kind of sexual involvement. She did admit to using coarse and earthy language and indulging in lewd jokes with Hannah, but to these two people this kind of verbal exchange was the norm. Zoe was summonsed to the presence of the area manager and soundly ticked off for exchanging vulgar jokes and remarks with a client. True, a home care assistant should probably preserve a certain distance between herself and the client, but nonetheless I felt very angry about the whole sorry episode and particularly incensed towards Greg, who had allowed himself to be hoodwinked by Hannah into accepting this defamation of Zoe's character. Moreover, this situation highlighted the dangers of stereotyping. It is probably not very wise to be influenced by theory and ideas to the extent that one can no longer see the wood for the trees.

Chapter Thirteen

Because the patch teams concentrated mainly on the over 65s, this was the age group with which I was heavily involved. Although each case had its unique features, an element in social work which prevents the job from ever becoming boring, the majority of cases were relatively low-key situations which could be resolved or at least alleviated by the provision of services such as respite care, meals-on-wheels, home care, etc, backed up by counselling the elderly people themselves and their relatives and friends.

Those who know little about social work with the elderly tend to think that it is a simple, straightforward matter which can be undertaken by anyone. They are unaware how much complex and diplomatic work is carried out not only with the old person himself but also with that person's wider circle. A year or two ago an acquaintance who was looking for a job irritated me profoundly when she said in dismissive tones: 'Oh, I could easily apply for a job like yours. The fact that I haven't any social work qualifications won't make any odds where the elderly are concerned.' I pointed out to her reasonably tactfully that when advertising for social workers, Social Services departments these days targeted only those with qualifications, regardless of client group.

Sometimes clients have no relatives or have lost touch with their families for a variety of reasons. One such client was Gertrude, who lived in one of the many council houses in Ashton. Over the years I have been inside many dirty houses, but perhaps the English language needs to acquire a new word with which to describe Gertrude's house. Filthy is scarcely adequate.

In her late 60s, Gertrude had recently lost her husband. According to her GP, he had died of TB and the specialist who had attended to the case felt the disease had been contracted because of the extremely unsanitary state of the house. Gertrude shared the house with several cats and dogs which were rarely let out. A large Alsatian was kept in the kitchen, where it urinated freely, and the floor quite literally oozed when walked upon. Several times the RSPCA had been called out by concerned neighbours, but it was clear that Gertrude was not ill-treating the animals and in fact had a very affectionate relationship with them. She was advised by the RSPCA that dogs must be regularly exercised.

Gertrude and her husband came originally from the South of England and had led a semi-nomadic life, moving from place to place. Since their arrival in -----shire they had inhabited a number of council houses, all of which had degenerated into horrendous hovels. One was declared by the Housing Department to be unfit for human habitation after the couple had been evicted for non-payment of rent. They had been living in Ashton for two or three years when a worried health visitor referred the case to us shortly after the husband's demise. In addition to the health and safety problems of a filthy person dwelling in a filthy house, Gertrude was also being taken advantage of financially by an unscrupulous neighbour who purported to be her 'carer' in return for a substantial part of her state pension, plus savings.

At this point I entered the scene. An occupational therapist who had visited Gertrude to assess for alterations to the house because Gertrude suffered from asthma and arthritis had only managed to stay in the house for five minutes. The stench and indescribable messes on every surface had triumphed over her professionalism. I wondered if I would be able to stand my ground any longer than that. Entering the house warily by the front door, left ajar, I found Gertrude sitting in a huddled attitude on what I guessed to be a sofa. It was covered with ancient rags, newspaper, bits of old food and a cat or two. I stood gingerly on one tiny piece of threadbare rug which did not appear to have any kind of offensive substance adhering to it. As I had walked from the door across to the rug, my shoes had stuck to the floor with every pace.

'Hello, Mrs M.,' I began, 'I heard about you from Mrs Wood, the health visitor, who said she was worried about you, so I came to see if there was anything I could do to help.'

Two surprisingly sharp black eyes scrutinised me from a haggard face, greyish-brown with grime. 'All I want is me 'usband back,' she replied. 'But you can't bring 'im back. No one can.'

There seemed to be no suitable reply to this, so I shifted my feet slightly on the minuscule corner of unsullied rug, and tried another tack. 'I understand you have a lot of pets, Mrs M. Would you like me to find someone who could take the dogs out for a walk?'

Gertrude continued staring at me out of her bright black eyes. 'No,' she said abruptly, 'me friend next door', and she jerked her head to the left, 'she takes the dogs out.'

I did not feel the interview was going very well. The invasive smell of decaying food, urine, unwashed human, dog and cat mess, and I dared not think what else, produced an overwhelming urge in me to quit the house as quickly as possible. I now knew what Anna, the occupational therapist, had felt like! Dimly aware that good social work practice would have been to encourage Gertrude to talk about her husband, I did not however do this, and started to blurt out rapid suggestions.

'Would you like someone to come and clean out your house? How about me helping you to sort out your finances? Perhaps one of our home care assistants could go shopping with you.'

Gertrude failed to respond to any of these suggestions. Hunched up in the corner of the sofa, she merely looked at me with unblinking eyes. I muttered goodbye, tottered over the sticky floor and almost fell through the front door and out into the weed-invaded front garden. For the rest of the day I could not stop washing my hands in an almost obsessional fashion. What, I wondered for the umpteenth time, made a person content to live in such conditions?

I had no idea what to do about Gertrude. A few days later I heard that she had arrived at the Accident and Emergency department of the local general hospital late on Saturday night, but the young doctor on duty was baffled. Gertrude had not had an accident and there did not appear to be an emergency situation. The nurses exclaimed over her dirt-encrusted clothes and one had apparently bluntly asked: 'When did you last see the inside of a bath?' Gertrude had stared back at her and retorted 'Bath? What's a bath?' They clearly had no more idea of what to do with Gertrude than I had. Eventually she was persuaded into being admitted to Winfield, the local psychiatric hospital, on a voluntary basis, where she stayed for a couple of weeks, thereafter returning to Ashton.

This cycle of events became a pattern. Gertrude would turn up at casualty, then be admitted to Winfield, then go home. After a while it became clear to me that she had a deep-seated dislike and fear of being alone, and this resulted in her appearances at hospital. The communal environment of a hospital met some basic need within her to be surrounded by people. During her relatively brief periods in her own home, Gertrude was increasingly dominated by her predatory next door neighbour, Sharon, who in theory was supposed to shop for her, provide her with some meals and keep on top of the chaos in Gertrude's house for which Gertrude paid her unjustifiably large sums. In actual fact Sharon did very little.

At one stage Gertrude spent four weeks in the assessment unit in Winfield. While she was there, I had several lengthy conversations with her, and she finally agreed that home care assistants should come in an attempt to clear up her house. I am usually of the opinion that people should be allowed to live in a dirty and chaotic condition if that is their chosen lifestyle, but Gertrude's lifestyle had started to impinge unpleasantly on other people. Rats, scavenging amongst the detritus in Gertrude's garden, were now being spotted in neighbouring gardens, and Gertrude's right hand neighbour (not Sharon) had complained to the council that she was unable to sell her house which had been on the market for nearly a year, because prospective buyers took one peep of consternation at the adjoining house and garden on their left, and were never seen again.

Sending in the home carers was not a success. With hindsight, I should not have expected them to tackle such a malodorous and unhygienic task. Even Christine, the patch carer, who did her fair share of scrubbing, disinfecting and attempting to sort through piles of often filthy rubbish and bric a brac, started to rebel.

However, just one of the home carers was determined to find a bright side to this sorry saga. Deirdre managed to strike up quite a good relationship with Gertrude and started bringing her hot meals from her own home as the grime-encrusted and urine-sprayed cooker in Gertrude's kitchen was unusable. Deirdre had her own highly individual thoughts about Gertrude and her lifestyle. 'This is how people must have lived in the Middle Ages,' she remarked to me one day. 'Gertrude's probably a throwback to those times, as she quite clearly thinks the way she lives is utterly normal.'

Gertrude would arrive home from her periods in hospital, and the tiny inroads that the home care assistants had made into the chaos were immediately undone by her slovenly habits. Following consultation with my senior, it was eventually decided that a firm of industrial cleaners should be employed. But even this team of workers only managed a superficial job. As with the home care assistants, Gertrude scuppered all their efforts every day by continuing to be as mucky and chaotically untidy as ever. Moreover, she failed to see anything wrong in allowing her pets to live in the same way.

The band of cleaners withdrew after a week of frustrating and unpleasant work, and the Social Services department was presented with a large bill. Having managed to secure a grant from the DSS, I bought Gertrude a bed as she had not slept in a bed for some years, merely dossing down on the filthy sofa in the living room. The beds upstairs were too dirty to use and indeed too rotten with damp to be slept in safely. Gertrude was as pleased as a small child with her new bed and clean bedding, obtained from the WRVS. However, needless to say, neither the bed nor the bedclothes remained clean for any length of time. We all seemed perpetually to return to square one with our efforts to help Gertrude. I suspected that she derived a certain amount of enjoyment and amusement from watching the various individuals and agencies striving to solve what they saw as problems with a marked lack of success.

Gertrude's original GP refused to keep her as a patient any longer (one could scarcely blame him, for apart from the state of the house and of Gertrude herself, she telephoned the surgery continually by day and night, demanding home visits), and two other local GP practices agreed to take it in turns to deal with her. Shortly after the failed clean-up initiative, Gertrude contracted a serious chest infection. Late one evening, Sharon called out the doctor whose turn it currently was to treat Gertrude, and who diagnosed pneumonia. She was despatched to hospital by ambulance.

While there, she and I had a lengthy discussion about the pros and cons of residential care. Gertrude acknowledged her need for constant company, and agreed to go to one of the local homes in Ashton for a few weeks as a way of finding out whether this sort of life was right for her. Privately, I had my doubts and was beginning to wonder if this square peg would ever fit into any hole.

It transpired, however, that this particular hole must have been created especially for Gertrude. She met her match in Maud, the home owner, a feisty Lancastrian who combined a no-nonsense firmness with a very genuine warmth. Maud agreed at once to take Gertrude on trial for a month, appearing totally undaunted by my frank and honest description of the situation. She laid down her ground rules to Gertrude, stating briskly that Gertrude could keep one of her cats, and that she would be responsible for its care and for keeping herself and her own room clean and tidy. The home's side of the bargain would be to befriend Gertrude and to make life for her as happy and comfortable as possible.

After a few initial hiccups characterised by some heated altercations between Gertrude and Maud – when the latter had occasion to reprimand Gertrude for such slovenly habits as throwing empty cat food tins on the floor instead on in the waste bin, or failing to attend to her personal hygiene – it became clear that Gertrude was settling down very well in this residential environment. Despite the fact that she was considerably younger than the majority of residents, she decided to stay for good.

The question of Gertrude's pets was answered by the efforts of the RSPCA and one or two animal-loving Ashton residents who managed to find good homes for them all. The

Housing Department swung into action and the filthy council house was quite literally scoured and fumigated from top to bottom, after which it emerged like a new building and was soon occupied by another tenant.

I was immensely relieved. The outcome of this incredibly difficult case was a favourable and, dared I say it, a successful one. Success is difficult to measure in social work and a word that social workers are wary of using. Above all else, I was relieved at the prospect of Gertrude being protected from Sharon's dishonest clutches. The elderly and the vulnerable of all age groups, not only children, are a prime target for abuse of all kinds, including financial abuse, and this is arguably the most challenging area of work with which Social Services staff have to grapple.

One might be forgiven for thinking that a small, remote town of this nature would consist overwhelmingly of an indigenous population. In the main, this was so, but I soon unearthed another, essentially alien, community scattered amongst the natives. These were Poles who had arrived in Ashton many years before as victims of the Nazis. They were now elderly and some were beginning to need help, due to frailty, from the public services, including our department. These original settlers, I soon discovered, mostly spoke no English, mixed only with each other, and focused their lives on the small Catholic church which they had built themselves not long after they arrived. Their children, the second generation, were mostly bilingual, whereas the grandchildren spoke only English and did not feel any affinity with Poland.

These Polish refugees had pitiful and tragic stories to tell (usually recounted to me by their English-speaking sons and daughters) of enforced deportation to Austria, Germany and other Nazi dominated countries, where they were compelled to toil on farms or in factories on starvation rations, before eventually travelling to Britain. During my time in the Ashton patch I felt tempted to treat these people as a special case because of their dark and terrible pasts.

Chapter Fourteen

All good things come to an end, including, eventually, the patch system. A change of director and most of senior management, with a consequent change of ideology, added to the fact that some patches were not operating successfully, led to the demise of this particular *modus operandi*. One or two patches had had no social worker attached to them for some time due to long-term sick leave or an unfilled vacancy. This meant that some vulnerable people received no assessments and no services while patch carers strove valiantly to cope with the less complex cases on their own.

When the patch system was done away with, some social workers were jubilant if they had disliked the area they worked in or had locked horns with their patch carer. I was not one of this joyful band, however. While working as a patch social worker I had felt really alive and had arrived at the conclusion that this way of working must surely be what social work was all about. I was quite devastated when the team manager announced that we were no longer to work in individual patches, but each social worker would take cases anywhere in the Eastbury area to ensure that the whole area was evenly covered by social work involvement. Did this mean that I would rarely go to that lovely sweep of country, that northernmost corner of rural -----shire? Would I be confined mainly to the housing estates of the town?

As the atmosphere in the town hall could frequently be described as uncongenial, I had tended to 'escape' into my patch. Office politics at the time were convoluted and unpleasant. In recent years there has been much publicity about bullying in the workplace, but this was the first time I had personally witnessed this disagreeable phenomenon, and I did not like what I saw. What took place was not the usual bullying or harassment of a more junior member of staff by a more senior member, but vice versa, the systematic persecution of a senior social worker by two field social workers.

What dark and turbulent events were taking place in the private lives of these social workers, or what had taken place in their murky pasts to cause them to react in this verbally sadistic way at work, heaven only knows. They tended to use the weekly team meeting as a forum at which they vented their derisive comments against the hapless victim. Everything she uttered, even the most innocent remark, they would pounce upon, tear to pieces and ridicule. She was obliged to act up and chair meetings for a time because of a temporary lack of team manager, and these bullies took advantage of this. Bullying children often resort to physical violence to taunt their victims, as well as verbal taunts, but the more sophisticated adult concentrates all his or her venom into words.

I started to dread the team meetings and felt most uneasy while they were actually taking place. Looking covertly around me, I could see that some of my colleagues were equally uneasy, and most of those present fell silent and gave up trying to take part in the discussion of the various agenda items.

This inexcusable unpleasantness only fizzled out when a different team manager took over chairing the meetings. I suspect that he was fully *au fait* with the situation for he did not allow the two persecutors to dominate the proceedings as they had done when the senior social worker was in charge in a temporary capacity. This was a classic instance of an unassertive person being targeted by two others with innate bullying tendencies who, in this case, resented the fact that she held a more senior position than they and considered her to be unfit for the post.

Blowing the whistle or bringing the problem into the open is always difficult, but if staff are aware of an unacceptable situation in a work setting, yet ignore it, the problem usually remains unresolved and those who chose to ignore it are left with lingering feelings of guilt. This is what happened to me. I still, several years later, feel dissatisfied with my failure to act.

Even though I no longer worked within a definite patch, I made it clear that I wished to work mainly in the more rural parts of the region. I was determined to retain that feeling of identity with a specific area which helped to compensate for the shortcomings of office life. The kaleidoscope was shaken once more. This time, approximately four social workers would be working in one of several designated areas, considerably larger than the original patches. After the unstructured method, which fortunately only lasted a short while, of dealing with cases everywhere and anywhere, there was once again going to be a definite pattern to our working lives. Things were looking up.

My area now included the small market town of Honeystone, a few miles from Eastbury, and the surrounding villages. As I gradually came to know this area, I arrived eventually at the conclusion that this change in my working pattern had its plus side. The new, enlarged patch was equally interesting and attractive and I was still able to operate in Ashton and its environs. Gone forever, however, was the system whereby each patch carer was directly accountable to a social worker; the patch carers' line managers were now the managers of the local authority residential homes. The weekly meetings, the lengthy telephone discussions, and the laughs and jokes exchanged by Christine and me were, regrettably, now but a memory, although we still saw each other from time to time.

No longer being responsible for a group of home care assistants represented for me a step back. Bit by bit we social workers were having our wings clipped and responsibilities taken away from us, which I found quite demeaning. Gone were the days of autonomy when each of us could make certain decisions regarding, for example, how many hours home care per week a client could be allocated. This became the responsibility of each team manager, who was now a budget holder. Senior management and the Social Services Committee had become paranoid about finance, and the director let it be known through the medium of the local paper that he considered social workers to be responsible for the lack of sufficient funds for home care because of their lavish and undisciplined allocation of home care hours to needy clients!

This we found deeply insulting. Yet again I found myself reflecting on the obvious fact that those at the top had very little knowledge or understanding of field social work and, like mediocre military officers, hid behind their front-line staff, blamed them for shortcomings that were more probably their own, and left it to the field workers to convey difficult messages to clients about departmental shortage of resources.

In a social services department, each layer of the hierarchy is supervised by the layer immediately above, from field level upwards. Who, I have from time to time wondered, supervises the elected members? God, perhaps? Because we social workers are regularly accountable to those above us, it seemed almost laughable that we should be portrayed in the local media as maverick freelance workers, dispensing largesse to needy members of the public with scant regard for a limited kitty.

Despite the drawbacks of operating within ever tighter constraints, I continued to find the work in my larger 'zone' challenging and interesting. Many of the cases and situations, particularly those out in the 'sticks', were unusual and the people involved often possessed colourful personalities.

Some miles from Ashton there lies a large, remote, scattered community consisting of farms, hamlets, old cottages, new bungalows, a few council houses, and a post office-cum-general store. Over the past ten years several clients dwelling in this area have come my way, one of whom was a lady in her 70s with learning difficulties, living on her own. She had been born and bred in the area and never lived elsewhere. For many years she and her brother shared a house, and when he died neighbours and other relatives pronounced darkly that Lizzie's future would be doomed if she tried to live alone.

'She'll never manage,' they all said. 'It'll be disastrous. She'll have to go into a home.'

But Lizzie had other ideas, and so did I, having already had some involvement with the case while her brother was still alive. Lizzie had the mind of a child, and she was unable to read or count, but some aspects of daily living she managed quite well unaided. She wished fervently to stay where she was, in the environment that had been familiar to her for over 70 years, and the mere thought of being made to become a resident in a home caused her to feel quite desperate. There were residential homes in both Ashton and Honeystone, but to Lizzie these small towns, although not more than ten miles away, were like a foreign country.

A home carer had already been assisting when brother and sister were together. I made it abundantly clear to all and sundry that Lizzie would continue to live in her own home with support from the Social Services and from her sister, who was a little younger than Lizzie and would assist her with taking a bath and with housework. It quite quickly became clear that Lizzie could function well in this way at home.

But this, unfortunately, was not the happy ending. Part of the home care assistants' task was to help Lizzie with her simple finances week by week. She could not, for example, distinguish a £5 note from a £10 note. However, the home carers became increasingly concerned by the fact that Lizzie's pension frequently seemed to dwindle puzzlingly fast, and they began to suspect that one or two of her 'friends' were taking advantage of the fact that Lizzie was unable to recognise numbers, and were persuading her to give them money. She would be unable to appreciate how much she was giving away. Both I and the two home carers involved in the case confronted, in a reasonably diplomatic fashion, various visitors to the house with our suspicions.

They retaliated by denying this hotly and claiming that Lizzie's sister, Meg, who lived about a mile along the road and trundled purposefully along the lane on her bike once or twice a week to 'do' for Lizzie, was behaving in a less than honest way with her sister's fiscal affairs. On her brother's death, Lizzie's finances had come under the control of the Court of Protection. Meg acted as 'receiver', which meant that she was responsible for collecting Lizzie's pension, dispensing it to her and dealing with other simple routine financial matters. Meg was accountable to the Court of Protection and on an annual basis was obliged to submit a detailed account of all her financial transactions on Lizzie's behalf. Because Meg, too, suspected several friends and neighbours of extracting money from Lizzie, she started giving Lizzie only part of her pension and various benefits every week, paying the rest into Lizzie's building society account. I never had any reason to disbelieve Meg or doubt her honesty.

In this remote rural community where everyone had known everyone else since the beginning of time, there erupted a furore. The community was split into two camps: those who backed Lizzie's 'supporters' and those – a minority – who sided with Meg. To compound an already complex situation, Meg and Lizzie, which they freely admitted themselves, had been at loggerheads with each other since childhood. Meg only helped Lizzie out of a sense of duty, not because of any feelings of sisterly love. Lizzie, in a simple child-like way, hugely enjoyed the fraught situation and tended to copy her 'supporters' and wag an accusing finger at her sister.

In the midst of this *melée* arose another figure, in the form of a self-appointed advocate. Mr Upton was a relative newcomer to the hamlet where Lizzie lived and had built himself an imposing semi-mansion some quarter of a mile from her council house. Evidently regarding himself as some kind of latter day village squire, Mr Upton quickly took it upon himself to 'oversee' the lives of his neighbours. His paternalistic eye soon alighted on Lizzie and he immediately came to the conclusion that because she had learning difficulties, she was in definite need of his benign intervention.

Advocacy is an excellent idea when undertaken by an appropriate individual or agency. Age Concern, for example, has an advocacy service whereby a member of their staff will act as advocate or mediator on behalf of a person who might be floundering in the midst of a complex situation and buffeted by conflicting interests. This is a helpful and positive service. Self-appointed advocates are another matter altogether, in my experience. Mr Upton turned out to be a nightmarish meddler who firmly believed he should take over the case.

He would telephone the office in Eastbury and demand to speak to me. In my absence he would speak at length to one of my colleagues, and sometimes remained on the line interminably. He appeared to imagine it was his God-given right to know everything about Lizzie and her affairs, and became angry and hectoring when I pointed out, between clenched teeth and with my nails digging into the desk to stop myself becoming less than courteous, that our department's involvement with Lizzie was strictly confidential. His particular hobby horse was an insistence that I should reveal every detail of Lizzie's financial situation to him, which I refused resolutely to do, as he was convinced that her sister was embezzling chunks of Lizzie's money. He also maintained that Lizzie was half-starved, and not fit to live on her own.

It transpired that Lizzie was invited quite frequently to Mr Upton's house, where he and his wife would ply her with substantial meals. Lizzie, like a gleeful and mischievous child, would slip into fantasy land and regale them with all kinds of colourful fibs about her sister. Lizzie was well known for her inability to stick to the truth, yet the Uptons drank in unquestioningly her stream of chatter.

Mr Upton demanded that a case conference be held to review the situation. I agreed to this, but refused point blank to let him attend the meeting on the grounds that confidential financial matters would be discussed. It was chaired by one of the senior social workers and took place in Lizzie's house. We sat around her humble kitchen table by the gently murmuring Aga, the panoramic landscape, so typical of the area, spread out like a giant quilt before us beyond the kitchen window.

Every now and again Lizzie's next door neighbour, Ted, would pop his head round the back door, survey the assembled company and say pointedly to Lizzie, with one raised enquiring eyebrow: 'Everything all right in here, Lizzie?' She, with an air of tremendous self-importance, would reply, 'Aye, everything all right, Ted.' Five minutes later, ponderous footsteps could be heard plodding along the garden path, and Ted's grizzled head would again appear round the door to herald a re-enactment of the scene. Probably Mr Upton had instructed Ted to check on the proceedings, and the latter was clearly taking this responsibility very seriously.

It was ascertained very clearly at the conference that Lizzie was managing well in her own home, had a good relationship with the home carers, and was well nourished. This last point was confirmed by the GP, who was at pains to point out that Lizzie was perhaps *too* well nourished and would benefit from a little weight loss.

After this the temperature cooled, the two 'camps' experienced a lull in hostilities, and life in that remote rural spot proceeded fairly smoothly. Meg and the home care assistants between them maintained a close vigil over Lizzie's money.

Then one dark December evening Dot, the home carer, called as usual to help Lizzie prepare for bed, but there was no one in the house. Going outside again, Dot stood in the garden and peered into the blackness. Had Lizzie hobbled next door with her curious rolling gait to visit Ted, as she sometimes did? Recently she had spent a fortnight in hospital after falling and injuring a leg, and needed an increased amount of help at home. Dot decided she had better knock on Ted's door.

She had taken a few steps towards Ted's house when she stumbled over something on the dark path. It was Lizzie, spread-eagled on the hard and frosty ground. She was dead.

The post mortem revealed that Lizzie had died of a heart attack. It was surmised that she had perhaps felt unwell and tried to seek Ted's help.

—o0o—

Within this sparsely populated outback there were some singular characters from all walks of life. Most were entirely indigenous, but a few were incomers from other parts of Britain, lured by the tranquillity and pastoral attractiveness of the area. One such was the late Nicholas Ridley, MP, well known for his xenophobic outbursts and anti-European sentiments, who took up residence in a grand house, and who did not endear himself to the locals by his refusal to allow them to use footpaths on his land.

One of our home care assistants who lived in the area worked privately as a cleaning lady for Mr Ridley. Leading up to his house was a long, tree-lined avenue. One day the woman happened to remark, as a polite way of making conversation while emptying the waste paper baskets, always full to the brim with fag ends and empty cigarette packets, that this attractive avenue, with its tree-lined approach, reminded her of country houses she had seen while on holiday in France.

Mr Ridley replied tersely: 'Bloody France? What connection do I want to have with bloody France!' End of conversation.

—o0o—

Dementia is sadly a predominant factor amongst many social services clients, yet a considerable number of those suffering from this condition manage to live in their own homes with varying degrees of support. Over the years I have dealt with many such clients, including Agnes who lived alone in a typical one-storey cottage. Some dementia sufferers are depressed and anxious, frightened because of the changes that their minds have undergone, but not Agnes. She was always chirpy, sociable, garrulous, and ready for a laugh. Her daughter and home carers came to help her twice, and on some days, three times daily, and she attended a local day centre for the elderly mentally infirm twice a week, though she was unable to retain any of this in her memory. Quite simply, everyday tasks she forgot how to do. In order to make a cup of tea, she would put a teabag in her handbag and squirt a dollop of tomato ketchup instead of milk into some unsuitable container such as a hot water bottle.

Agnes had always loved dogs and sometimes told me about dogs her family had owned when she was a child. She could recall with reasonable accuracy events and facts of long ago, and once confessed to me that she had always preferred dogs to children. Her cottage backed onto open fields, in the nearest of which resided a goat which Agnes enjoyed watching from her living room window. However, she did not see it as a goat, but was quite convinced that this bearded, skittish creature rambling over the green sward was her favourite animal, a dog.

One wild, stormy October evening Agnes went out into the field behind the house, stumbling over ruts and furrows, and led the goat back into her garden, down the path, and into the warmth of the house. 'Dogs like to be indoors when the weather's bad,' she said to herself. She let the goat have the run of the house, and it wandered quite happily in and out of the bedroom, kitchen and bathroom, and back into the living room, chewing a curtain here and crunching up a toothbrush there, not to mention laying waste to a pile of underwear lying on Agnes's bed.

The following morning Bella, the home care assistant, arrived as usual at breakfast-time. A startling, messy, and smelly scene greeted her bemused gaze as she stepped through the front door. A moment later she was almost pinned to the wall in the hall as some kind of creature hurtled past her and out into the garden. Peering after it, she saw to her astonishment that it was a goat. The state of the house was almost beyond description. Goat droppings were in every room, and clothes and other items that the animal had chewed or half eaten were strewn about chaotically. In the midst of this sat Agnes, in her usual chair in the living room, smiling serenely. She appeared to be unaware of the mess and chaos, and told Bella that she had given a poor dog a home for the night.

As soon as Bella had sufficiently recovered from her initial stunned reaction, she telephoned her line manager at her office base in one of the Ashton residential homes. By this time the home care staff were being supervised by the residential home managers. She also contacted Agnes's long-suffering daughter, who drove post-haste to her mother's cottage where she was obliged to tackle the mammoth task of clearing up the house. The goat was placed in another field, out of sight of the house. The residential home manager telephoned me at the office to inform me of this latest incident amongst my caseload, and could scarcely speak for laughing. There were in fact few straight faces to be seen around the office as this story circulated.

A telephone call also came in later from Agnes's daughter, who certainly was not laughing. I think this latest escapade of her mother's nearly defeated her. Often, where cases of dementia are concerned, it is the relatives who suffer most and need as much – if not more – support and sympathy than the actual client. Informal carers vary tremendously in the quality of care they give and in the way they co-operate or fail to co-operate with 'officials' involved in the case, such as social workers, district nurses, etc. A significant number, for many different reasons, are not, unlike Agnes's daughter, a positive element in the lives of their frail, elderly relatives, and are certainly sent to try the patience, tolerance and diplomatic skills of social workers.

Chapter Fifteen

The year 1993 was a significant one in the lives of Social Services staff. As part of the parliamentary community care changes and reforms, financial responsibility for residential and nursing home care shifted from the DSS to the Social Services. Prior to 1993 those elderly needing care and wishing to enter privately run homes but unable to afford the full fee were automatically funded by the DSS. Superficially, the purse looked to be bottomless, but in reality, of course, no purse has a magic bottom.

Those of us who had worked with the elderly for many years were well used to liaising with residential staff, but this was largely within the sphere of local authority homes. As the years of the 1980s rolled by, the growth in the number of private homes gathered momentum. From April 1993 a considerable chunk of our time was spent negotiating with home owners and managers, and also explaining at length to elderly clients and their families that strict eligibility criteria had to be applied, as well as a means test. Not only private care homes, but also local authority run homes were included in this scheme.

In both Ashton and Honeystone, areas where I mainly worked, there are two private residential homes and one local authority home, plus a nursing home (all nursing homes are private) near Honeystone. There is often a great deal of rivalry, resentment and suspicion detectable between the private and public sectors, and in the midst of this cauldron of ruthless competition and sometimes unfriendly vibes are the social workers, swimming cautiously in the murky soup and attempting (sometimes unsuccessfully) to play a totally neutral role.

Added to this often fraught scenario arose the ever increasing scarcity of home care, day care, and meals-on-wheels. We now found ourselves telling clients what they would have to go without rather than what they could have. This is not a role I relished; I had not taken up a career in social work in order to say to vulnerable people: 'I'm sorry, I see very well what you need, but you can't have it because the resources are lacking.' Some clients took out their frustration and dismay on the social worker sitting or standing before them. The social worker at the other end of a telephone line is also sometimes used as a convenient punchbag. One of the hardest aspects of the job is being obliged always to remain polite in the face of verbal abuse. Social workers have feelings too!

These feelings have to be vigorously suppressed when dealing with daughters such as Mrs O, who held me captive on the telephone at the end of one Friday afternoon when I had spent the entire day wresting with one difficult case after another.

With a hint of menace in her voice, she declared that she had a journalist friend who would be more than willing to publish a nice little story in one of our local papers about our lack of resources in general and about her very elderly mother in particular, who was not yet in receipt of all the services that the daughter was demanding. 'Three months my mother's had to wait, three months! It's a disgrace.'

Mrs O then went on to declare that she could not understand why 'all these foreigners' who arrived in Britain in droves obtained benefits and other services straight away while decent English people like her mother had to wait endlessly. I felt I could not let this pass without comment and pointed out as courteously as possible that the majority of asylum seekers are fleeing from nightmarish political and economic circumstances and deserved our compassion, whereupon Mrs O retorted that she was a Christian woman and therefore did not need anyone to tell her about compassion. Yet again I wondered despairingly whether these so-called Christians ever read the New Testament.

I felt obliged to warn my long-suffering team manager of this particular piece of blackmail, so that the possibility of unsavoury 'facts' being splashed across the front page of next Friday's local paper would not come as too much of a shock. He heaved a weary sigh and highlighted the fact that Mrs O's mother had been funded for certain basic services within a week or two of assessment and that many clients were obliged to wait longer than three months. The majority of clients do indeed wait patiently and with understanding, appreciating the difficulties with which the Social Services department has to grapple.

Needless to say, Mrs O's mother was granted funding for extra services at the next home care panel meeting, presumably because the panel members felt unable to take the risk of unpleasant media publicity. This type of blackmail on the part of some (mercifully few) clients or relatives never fails to rile social workers and their managers. People who approach their MP or who telephone HQ demanding to speak to the director usually succeed in triggering a knee-jerk reaction so that their particular case jumps to the head of a long queue, regardless of the urgency of the situation.

Another example of 'thorn-in-the-side' relatives was the singularly obnoxious man who talked non-stop at me down the telephone for nearly 40 minutes, reviling me and several other workers involved in the case. We were not fit to walk upon the earth, it would appear, and all because he was adamant that his mother-in-law should be stashed away in a home or incarcerated in a psychiatric hospital, when it was clear to us that she was quite capable of living in her own home! This same relative dominated an ensuing case conference, during which he proclaimed his superior knowledge of mental illness, despite the fact that three medically qualified people were present at the conference. Once again, one had to resort to the digging of one's nails into the table in order to refrain from a less than courteous retaliation.

A few days later, a telephone discussion of this case took place between me and Nathalie, one of the nurses who had attended the case conference.

'He's so preposterous that he's almost a joke!' declared Nathalie, referring to the aforementioned relative. Well, maybe, but working life would be less irksome without such almost jokes.

Thankfully, most of the general public are quite different. Down the years I have felt sometimes almost humbled by instances of elderly people, their families, friends and neighbours enduring hardship and problems of mountainous proportions who have at the same time been capable of perceiving that Social Services staff are striving manfully (or womanfully) to provide assistance against a backdrop of dwindling resources. Those people who say a quiet 'thank you' to a social worker when he or she has managed to bring about some positive good are the ones who enable social workers to feel they are willing to battle on a little longer.

One of the most valuable and essential social work skills is the ability to communicate with every type of human being in an open-minded and non judgemental way. Putting this high-minded concept into practice is sometimes far from easy. Every type includes every conceivable layer of social class, and also a variety of sexual orientations and gender. Over the years I have come across several instances of elderly homosexuals, both men and women, who have felt obliged to spend their entire lives concealing their sexual tendencies from the wider community. In some cases, couples have moved many hundreds of miles from their roots, families and friends in order to be together in an area where they were not known. When those gays who are now elderly were young adults, a sexual relationship between two people of the same sex was still illegal. But being together did not mean sharing a house in an open manner like the majority of heterosexual couples. It meant living in separate abodes and not meeting too frequently for fear of 'society' guessing their secret. What does this say about our society? I consider it a privilege that the elderly gays I have met have felt able to talk to me about their sexuality and their partners. Sometimes this was the first and only occasion they talked to someone who was not from the gay community.

As for social background, I found my resolve to approach everyone with an attitude of tolerance (there are exceptions, of course – one cannot help but have a judgemental attitude towards those who abuse, for example) somewhat tested when a case involving members of an aristocratic family came my way. One's own personal views, prejudices and political leanings inevitably play a part when dealing with clients, and one has to sit on these quite firmly and look upon the people involved as human beings in need, whether they be dukes or dustmen, or anyone in between.

In this particular case, my own colleagues had expressed some negative criticism. Even my team manager ventured to say: 'Are we really here to provide a service for the aristocracy?' One of the medical staff at the hospital where the noble elderly lady was an inpatient even went so far as to declare she felt strongly tempted to withhold her services altogether. I firmly pointed out that this lady and her son had become impoverished through no fault of their own, and that she was eligible for Social Services and NHS care and assistance. However, I have to confess that I struggled to believe my own utterance!

A case conference was held at the hospital to thrash out plans for the client's future care. I found this experience so fascinating that I almost forgot to make my contribution to the conference. The lady's son was evidently so keen to play down his aristocratic lineage and demonstrate that he was really 'one of the people' that he appeared at the meeting wearing grubby trainers and a T-shirt that had seen better days. The nurse representing the medical staff at the meeting was resolutely determined to ignore the fact that her patient emanated from a 'different' background from that of the bulk of patients passing through the hospital, and referred throughout to 'your mum' when explaining the likely prognosis and various medical procedures to the son. I have been present at and indeed chaired many case conferences over the years, but this one stands out in my memory as being peculiarly bizarre and comical at the same time.

The eventual outcome was the lady's admission to a residential home, where she settled down quite well, but before that various home care services were put in place in an attempt to enable the client to remain in her own home. This entailed several visits to the ancestral pile, the size and grandeur of which contrasted oddly with the sparsely furnished council house or the minimalist possessions of isolated cottage dwellers from which I had usually just driven.

The son was contemptuous of the small amount of home care we were able to provide, which admittedly did not meet his mother's needs. Round-the-clock care was the only solution. This at first took the form of private care at home, for which the client had to pay. Even this intensive package of care proved insufficient, and she was eventually admitted into residential care.

However, the work had to go on, despite the multiple drawbacks. I continued to travel in remote realms and deal with a mixed bag of cases. Often the only people living and working in the more far-flung areas were farmers, many of whose families had farmed in the same place for generations. They grew old and clung tenaciously to the land and the farmhouse, or they died and their widows or other relatives grew old and frail and were clearly struggling, although most refused to admit this. Many were extremely reluctant to spend any money despite the fact that they had amassed considerable sums.

Of course, there were exceptions. Some were singular personalities and would probably be described as originals. Some had never married and run the farm with a bachelor brother or nephew. One case I dealt with was an unmarried farmer in his 70s who had managed the family farm for many years with his brother, but who had had both legs amputated due to a circulatory disease. Confined to a wheelchair, he was looked after devotedly by his brother, supported by daily visits from a home care assistant. The idea of residential care for the amputee never entered the heads of either of them, despite the small amount of home care support we could give.

Whenever I arrived at the farm, jolting and bumping over the ruts in the narrow lane, I would be greeted by the sight of at least a dozen cats of every hue, shape and size, sunning themselves on the cobbles and observing the arrival of my car with that air of laid back curiosity which only cats can affect. The elderly brothers were well acquainted with the quirks of personality of every cat, each of which possessed a name from yesteryear such as Mathilda or Ethelred.

The majority of the farms inhabited by the elderly looked as if they belonged to a bygone era which, indeed, they did. Completely devoid of modernisation, one stepped into another age once past the threshold, with massive kitchen dressers and enormous, solid tables and the inevitable grandfather clock or two, dark and sombre-looking. Most of these houses were reasonably clean, but one exception was a tumbledown farm belonging to Mrs D, a very old lady, and her bachelor son, the latter resembling some biblical character with a black beard stretching nearly to his waist. The ancient mother was in her late 90s, at least she thought this was her probable age! Neither she nor anyone else knew her exact age; at the local GP's surgery, beside the entry 'Date of Birth' on her medical records there stood a question mark instead of a date!

Deirdre, the home care assistant who had befriended Gertrude in her filthy house in Ashton, would have had some interesting comments to make about this farm. A medieval air it certainly possessed on account of its extreme dirtiness and also because of the starkly plain, sparse and ancient items of furniture. I was usually asked to take a seat when I visited, but always declined with some hastily concocted excuse. The one startling, jarring note in this scene from the Middle Ages was the huge, all-dominating TV screen in a corner of the living room.

Because of the ever worsening financial situation, Mrs D could not be given more than half an hour's daily home care. This was clearly insufficient, but she and her son resolutely refused to supplement this by spending money on private care, although I knew, once again through the local bush telegraph, that they had plenty stashed away, totally unused, in savings accounts.

One morning, at about 10am, the home carer arrived to be greeted by a wild-eyed son stumbling around in the farmyard. 'Mother's still asleep, all cold and stiff. I can't waken her.' He clutched at Bella's arm.

Mrs D had, at long last, slipped away in the night and left this world. Her poor son simply could not grasp that his mother was dead. He had probably convinced himself that she was immortal. They had, after all, shared a home for over 60 years.

Sometimes elderly women are left in charge of farms when their menfolk have passed away. An example of this was Mrs J, who had been a widow for many years. Her daughter, her only child, and her son-in-law had been killed together in a car crash, leaving their two young children orphans. They were taken in and eventually adopted by relatives in another county on the father's side. The little girl had been born with quite severe learning difficulties and her older brother, who was quite normal, was fiercely protective of his sister.

Mrs J was a grimly determined lady of nearly 90 with a strong, dogged personality. She had been running the farm single-handed since her husband's death, with help of a casual nature from a farm hand who turned up when he felt like it. She liked to have her grandchildren to stay as often as possible, which was sometimes difficult to arrange as relations between her and the children's legal guardians were somewhat strained.

They were both well into their teens when I started visiting the farm, which I had been asked to do by Mrs J's GP, who was becoming increasingly dubious about her capacity to deal with the granddaughter who, at the age of 14, possessed the mind and behaviour of a toddler. Both were at risk, the doctor felt, because Mrs J had become too old and infirm to be able to cope with this sadly defective grandchild. However, Mrs J hotly denied that she was 'past it'. As I gradually grew to know her and became familiar with the situation, I realised that she still saw herself as a vigorous, active 25-year-old who was well able to run the farm and the house with one hand and look after her granddaughter with the other. In reality she was quite frail with arthritic knees, and could only hobble fairly slowly.

Like most farms I became acquainted with, Mrs J's farmhouse was old-fashioned in the extreme, with the usual heavy, brooding furniture, housed in dark, gloomy rooms. In common with most of her generation of farming folk, she shared the house with a considerable army of mice, which she considered to be quite a normal situation. The fact that the mice wrought an alarming amount of damage in every room and left a trail of droppings in the kitchen bothered her not one iota. Her greatest passion was baking, and every week she would bake batches of cakes, her favourite being enormous fruit cakes. It never seemed to occur to her that there was no one beside herself to eat these goodies, which were piling up in the pantry. No one, that is, apart from the mice who were, of course, delighted with this gargantuan feast.

Eventually we arrived at a compromise regarding Caroline, the granddaughter. She could come to stay at the farm provided Matthew, her brother, came with her and helped look after her. By this time Matthew was a bright young university student, so visits to the farm could only be arranged during his vacations. I met him several times and never failed to be impressed by his clear-cut feelings of responsibility towards his handicapped sister. There were frequently moments of discord and tension between him and his grandmother. 'A veritable chip off the old block,' I found myself thinking, for Matthew and his grandmother were strikingly alike in character – very strong willed, not to say domineering.

Matthew often had critical comments to make about the state of the house and about his grandmother's lifestyle. The fact that she only took a bath once a week particularly incensed him. He tried to persuade me to tell the old lady that this was not acceptable from a hygienic point of view, and I was at pains to point out to him that the modern habit of taking a daily bath or shower did not apply to his grandmother's generation.

At first Mrs J was relatively frosty towards me but as time went by she unbent and talked to me at length about her family, her past, and her concerns regarding her two grandchildren, who were the apple of her eye and her *raison d'être*. Matthew, she instinctively realised, was a survivor and would make his way in the world, probably quite successfully. But Caroline was another matter altogether. Mrs J brooded continually over Caroline's possible future. As far as I was able, I attempted a little bridge-building between the old lady and the children's other relatives who did not communicate directly with each other but appeared to use Matthew as a messenger boy. Mrs J was typical of her generation of farmers in that she could scarcely conceive of a world outside the farming circle. In her mind's eye there seemed to lodge a picture of her beloved granddaughter in the clutches of uncaring people who inhabited the alien world of the urban Midlands.

On the contrary, it seemed to me that Caroline's needs were being properly catered for. She attended a special school for children with learning disabilities, but otherwise lived at home with her adoptive parents, apart from occasional periods of respite care when they went on holiday or needed a break from the exhausting business of caring for a handicapped child. I explained all this to Mrs J and attempted to reassure her that Caroline would not be cast out alone into a harsh world once she had left school. Mrs J remained largely unconvinced, and was clearly determined to keep herself going physically and mentally so that she could continue to play a definite part in caring for Caroline.

However, the months passed and Mrs J's health deteriorated. Because by this time the Social Services home care assistants were no longer carrying out practical tasks such as housework or shopping, I had had to persuade Mrs J to employ and pay a private home help to come and attempt to clean the rambling old house and to relinquish our home care assistant who had been working for Mrs J for some years. Trying to tackle that house was in fact beyond the scope of any home help. A never-ending stream of women working for the private agency were all defeated by the cluttered rooms and continual patter of tiny mouse feet.

The GP urged Mrs J to consider residential care, but this concept was as alien to her as the urban world inhabited by her grandchildren. Outraged, she sent the good doctor packing.

'A home!' she remarked to me. 'Dr D wants me to go into a home.' She made the word sound as if it were something truly disgusting, as if the doctor had uttered an obscenity.

Due to heart problems, Mrs J was admitted to the nearby hospital for investigations. This was to be her final resting place on this earth, for she suffered a heart attack while in hospital and died soon after.

Many questions were left unanswered. I have never found out what happened to Caroline, who certainly would have been bewildered by her grandmother's death. I suspect that the farm was left to Matthew, but to this day I am in the dark as to what has become of it. Matthew told me that he did not wish to enter the farming world; an ambitious young man, he had acquired a degree in business studies and had his sights set on the heady world of modern wheeling and dealing.

It was not always the farmer's widow who was left to grow old by herself on the farm; other family members living and working there, such as nephews, sometimes found they had arrived at middle age and were saddled with the responsibility of caring for an ageing relative. Or perhaps *not* caring for them, as the case may be.

On a remote farm, some miles from Ashton, which took me the best part of an hour to reach from the centre of Eastbury, there lived an elderly woman in her 80s with her nephew, aged about 40. In theory, Jack, the nephew, ran the farm, but in reality he did little and all the hard graft was left to his brother, who also had a farm a mile or so away. Jack was a strange, dour man of few words who spent a large part of the day sitting at the kitchen table smoking while Dolly, his aunt, tottered slowly around making cups of tea and generally waiting on him.

I soon gave up trying to drive right up to the farm, after my engine stalled on one occasion as I attempted to urge the car back up the steep track towards the road. It was a gloomy, icy December afternoon and the dusk was gathering fast. At first I feared I would stay marooned on this lonely slope until I became an icicle, but at last the engine spluttered into life again and the car lurched forward. Thereafter I donned my wellies and left my car on the road, walking the final half mile to the farm buildings.

Jack had a rather unnerving habit of lurking in one of the many ramshackle outbuildings and emerging slowly just as I approach the farmyard.

'Hello, Jack. Things all right?' I would enquire, feeling vaguely uneasy and also somewhat foolish as I stumbled over the ruts and stones in my bright red boots, trying not to drop my handbag and case into the ever-present mud.

Jack, a very thin man of medium height, would stare at me unsmilingly.

'Aye, all right, I s'ppose,' he would reply after a long pause.

Following this ritual exchange of pleasantries, I would climb the steps which led into the scullery-cum-storeroom and then the kitchen. This was yet another example of an old farmhouse set fast in a time warp. The kitchen where Dolly and Jack seemed to spend all their time was chaotic in the extreme, with an ancient Aga nudging shoulders with the battered wooden table, perpetually strewn with half-used jars of marmalade, old newspapers, tins of evaporated milk and crusts of bread.

Dolly was a tiny, bird-like woman, with an almost whispering voice, who looked so frail that I feared she might crumble away if knocked. Her appetite was likewise tiny, and the district nurses tried to feed her up by encouraging her to consume special fortified drinks, full of vitamins and protein. These she always accepted politely, but we all suspected that she rarely drank them. Whenever I visited, Dolly would offer me one of these special drinks on the grounds that I did such a strenuous job, I must need fortifying!

For a while she managed quite well with daily home care visits and twice weekly attendance at a day centre in Ashton. But as time went on she grew gradually more frail and more unsteady on her feet. She was quite literally tottering from crisis to crisis, suffered several bad falls, and was admitted to hospital in Eastbury, then discharged home again, gradually fading. She clung to the conviction that it was her role to wait on Jack and generally look after him. She explained to me that he had always been a strange boy who had never made friends, and this worried her continually.

Fortunately Dolly had an excellent GP from a practice in a neighbouring county, for whom nothing was too much trouble. For some reason Jack was registered with a different practice, but he refused ever to see a doctor. Dolly's GP suspected he was severely depressed, and felt the situation had reached the point where it was too risky for Dolly to continue living on this tumbledown farm with a depressed and useless nephew. He and I decided to meet at the farm one afternoon together with the district nurse.

We gathered round the chipped and scored kitchen table, laden as usual with tins of evaporated milk *et al*, Jack at one end in his usual chair with his back to the window, and Dolly at the other end in her sagging old armchair. Through the grubby window panes could be glimpsed the almost unbearably lovely landscape of the region – giant meadows, wooded hillsides and that near palpable tranquillity. As I glanced round at the assembled company, it struck me that this strongly resembled a scene from 'Dr Finlay's Casebook'. Dolly and Jack had always shared the house with a variety of livestock, and during the meeting a cockerel wandered in and out, sometimes accompanied by several hens. The elderly collie slumbered noisily by the Aga, while a small tortoiseshell cat gnawed at some stale crusts placed on a saucer by the window. While we debated and pondered, the cockerel strutted and clucked around the table, apparently wishing to join in and give its opinion, and now and again giving the dog and cat a sharp tap with its beak.

The outcome of this meeting was that Dolly agreed, albeit reluctantly, to try residential care. Some days later she was conveyed to a residential home in Honeystone. A few weeks' trial lengthened into months. Dolly became ever weaker and was declared to be terminal by two doctors. However, she duped them all and lingered on for another two years before expiring as quietly as she had lived. During her twilight years in Honeystone, Dolly's mind did not remain totally intact, but she remembered the farm very clearly and often spoke to me about it in her whispering voice.

'I'm just staying in this place for a while until I'm better,' she informed me, while I bent low over her chair to catch her words. 'Come the Spring, I'll be back up there for the lambing.'

From time to time Jack came to see her, in his stained and ragged farm clothes, and would sit awkwardly by her side looking like a fish out of water, or rather a rustic divorced from his byre, in this clean, orderly and brightly decorated home. Always a man with a paucity of words, he became totally silent when visiting his aunt, and scarcely managed to mutter 'thank you' when handed a cup of tea by one of the friendly staff.

I heard from Jack's brother that nothing changed on the farm. Jack continued to wander vaguely around the buildings and fields, the old collie ambling at his heels, while his brother toiled anxiously in an effort to maintain two farms in that remote and exquisite corner of Northern England.

Chapter Sixteen

Back at the ranch – the ranch in this case being the town hall in Eastbury – working life was just as busy as it was out in the field. Several hours every day, whether we liked it or not, we were chained to our desks with the telephone clamped to one ear, and a heap of files, wads of forms, memos and other miscellaneous pieces of paperwork strewn over every square inch of the desk.

Surrounded as I was by items of modern technology, I reluctantly came to the conclusion that I would have to try and initiate myself into the working methods of the late twentieth century. Easier said than done, as I think I was probably born with the portion of one's brain that deals with technology entirely missing. Along with a clutch of other cowering technophobes in the office, I put off for as long as possible the, to me, nigh impossible step of sitting in front of a computer screen and attempting to withdraw information from it.

Even the photocopier presented me with insurmountable problems. During my time in Fairfield, photocopiers were first introduced into the Social Services offices, and I attained the dubious distinction of being the only member of staff who never really grasped how this gobbling, spewing monster, complete with high pitched beeps and winking lights, actually operated.

However, a photocopier was a trivial matter compared with a computer. I realised that the evil day could be put off no longer when it was firmly announced that all social work staff would undergo some compulsory basic training in computing. The person in charge of the IT training section at Social Services headquarters quite rightly took her job very seriously, and maintained that all staff members, however terrified and/or incompetent, were capable of mastering the basics, especially when supplied with an idiots' guide to elementary computing. However, it had probably not occurred to her that the world also contains super idiots.

During our compulsory training day, one of the hurdles to be addressed was the mystifying jargon surrounding IT. The trainer came to the word 'icon' and enquired whether we understood the meaning. Unthinkingly, I announced brightly that an icon is something connected with the Russian Orthodox church. For the rest of the day, the trainer's clearly visible fight to suppress her irritation and impatience must have caused an alarming rise in blood pressure. Many years before that, as a small schoolgirl aged about seven, I had brought about a similar reaction in my arithmetic teacher by informing her that of course a pound of feathers would weigh less than a pound of potatoes. Mathematics, like IT, was another area of black mystery to me.

On the positive side I, together with a colleague, took part in a tentative project known as GP liaison. It was becoming increasingly recognised in health and social care circles that the NHS and Social Services needed to work more closely together, not only as regards pooled budgets but to try and heal the rift between the two professions that, historically, had resulted from hostility due mainly to ignorance of each other's ways of working and *Weltanschauung*.[2] This did not mean, of

---

2 German word meaning 'philosophy of life' or 'way of looking at the world.'

course, that all employees within the two public services were perpetually warring with each other; on the contrary, many individual nurses, doctors and other medical and paramedical staff have for decades liaised effectively in a friendly manner with Social Services staff.

My colleague and I met once a month with one of the GPs from the Honeystone practice for informal discussion of issues of importance, both local and national, to both professions. The word 'informal' is probably a euphemism – sitting comfortably with mugs of coffee with no agenda, no minutes taken, and no note-book constituted a pleasant contrast to the usual hectic formal working life of all three of us. At first I attempted to introduce an element of formality into the proceedings by bringing my large desk diary with me and jotting down a few notes, but sensible Dr L would have none of this, and I soon learnt to leave my diary behind.

Another project in which I took part – this time more formal with an agenda, minutes and guest speakers – was attendance, four times per year, at the practitioners' forum. This was a get-together of frontline workers from all over the county with the aim of discussing, criticising and attempting to improve the working lives of frontline practitioners, not always welcome ways of working imposed on us by those above us in the hierarchy. Sometimes we indulged in a general moaning session which certainly had a cathartic effect, but usually the discussions were constructive and positive. On the whole we had a very clear concept of how we should be working in order to give an effective service to clients, but felt shackled and frustrated due to over-large caseloads, virtually non-existent resources, and a constant stream of government initiatives which we workers on the ground were expected to put into practice in addition to the grind of our everyday work.

How to convey these conclusions upwards to senior managers proved to be a daunting struggle, but after a year or two it became clear that those at the top were beginning to take notice of the minutes of the forums. In all fairness to senior management, they have little choice when it comes to implementation of government edicts; they feel duty bound to instruct frontline staff to carry these out.

On one occasion our director came to address the forum, and afterwards there took place a lively question and answer session. The number of years I had spent in the world of social work and how social mores had changed since those far-off youthful days in Sheffield was brought home forcibly to me when I suddenly became aware that a social worker from the 'floor' was addressing the director as Colin. On hearing this I started involuntarily and began to reflect that it would have been unthinkable all those years ago even to have addressed the team leader by his first name, let alone the person at the apex of the hierarchy! So much for the swinging 60s! Our team leader at the Social Care department in Sheffield, Mr L, a devout Catholic who used to spend every lunch break on his knees in the pro-cathedral praying for his motley flock of social workers, did not, as far as I was concerned, even possess a Christian name. None of us, I suspect, ever knew what it was. As for my present director, I was probably still too inhibited ever to address him as anything other than Mr Timpson.

An altogether more congenial experience was that of student supervision. Over a period of years I acted as study supervisor to several Social Services staff undergoing various social work or social care training courses. I discovered that there is possibly nothing more satisfying than observing someone making progress, eventually completing a course and acquiring a qualification, and knowing that you played a definite part in this successful development. A one-to-one relationship with a student was my forte, I found; dealing with a class or group would probably not have been so congenial to me.

In-service training courses took place at regular intervals and comprised a wide variety of topics, ranging from information-giving courses on subjects such as dementia, to how to cope with stress in the workplace. I have been attending in-service training courses for over 20 years and have little recollection of the bulk of them, which either points to an incapacity for factual retention on my part, or indicates a certain mediocrity about the courses themselves. Whatever the reason, there are some topics about which I feel strongly and on which there have been useful training courses, particularly those relating to adult abuse.

The abuse of adults is a phenomenon which has only recently started to emerge from the murky depths of concealment and enter the limelight. Like abuse against children it is probably an age-old evil, but has been denied and kept under very thick wraps until relatively recently. The elderly, those with mental health problems, people of all ages with physical handicaps, and those with learning difficulties are all vulnerable and in need of protection, just as children are. They are just as likely to be abused by those in charge of them. Is there a National Society for the Prevention of Cruelty to Adults? I have never heard of one, yet there has been a pressing need for a countless number of years.

Cruelty and abuse can take many forms. Social workers come across every variety in the course of their work, but it is often very difficult to prove. Sometimes a relative is physically abusing a frail elderly person and perpetrating other types of abuse, such as financial, at the same time. One extraordinary case I dealt with concerned an elderly man, Mr T, who had suffered a stroke, and who was also exhibiting probable symptoms of Parkinson's, although the doctors were finding this very difficult to diagnose. He lived in an isolated cottage and his adult granddaughter lived next door, or at least she did in theory – in actual fact she had moved in with her grandfather. A home carer started visiting morning and evening to help the granddaughter get Mr T up and put him to bed. It was not long before I started receiving worrying reports from the home care assistant. Mr T also attended the day care facilities at the cottage hospital in Honeystone, and the nurses there expressed their concern over some unexplained bruising on various parts of Mr T's body.

According to the home carer the granddaughter, Pat, treated her grandfather very roughly. The latter's bedroom was situated at the far end of a long passage which had to be traversed in order to reach the living room. Because of his physical disabilities, Mr T was scarcely mobile and could only put one foot in front of another with painful slowness while leaning heavily on his zimmer. It took the best part of half an hour for him to walk the length of the corridor in the morning and again in the evening when returning to his bedroom. While this distressing journey was taking place, Pat would walk behind her grandfather shouting rudely at him and aiming little kicks at the back of the zimmer.

Pat was immune to remonstrations on the part of the home care assistant and also discussions with me. Responding to the concern expressed, I visited Pat and her grandfather several times and suggested to Pat that she could borrow a wheelchair from the hospital so that her grandfather could be wheeled from bedroom to living room or, at the very least, Mr T should have the opportunity to rest at intervals on a chair brought out into the passage for that purpose.

Stubbornly Pat insisted that elderly people needed to be kept moving, otherwise they seized up altogether, and that she had observed the physiotherapists working with her grandfather in hospital and was merely using their methods of firm encouragement. As for the bruises, she maintained that her grandfather fell sometimes which inevitably caused bruising. But that did not explain away the persistent purple weals behind the knees or on the ankles, or the angry red marks on his face.

Mr T himself was an almost silent person who communicated little with those trying to help him. On being encouraged to talk about his home life, he refused to criticise his granddaughter and his face took on the look of a frightened rabbit if he felt we were becoming too insistent. Pat, who was recently divorced, had acquired a boyfriend who lived most of the time in Mr T's house. I strongly suspected that he played an active role in this sinister scenario. By living largely in her grandfather's house, Pat was able to save a considerable amount of money as all household expenses – fuel and telephone bills, etc – were paid for out of her grandfather's pension and various DSS benefits. This in itself amounted to financial abuse, in my view.

Because the family's GP refused to believe that Pat, whom he had known since she was a child, was physically chastising her grandfather, verbally harassing him or helping herself to large amounts of his money, I decided to tackle the consultant over the GP's head. This GP was a classic example of the majority of people who bury their heads in the sand and deny that abuse of the elderly takes place.

The consultant who had been seeing Mr T in Honeystone was an entirely different kettle of fish. He himself was concerned about Mr T and well aware of the potential for abuse. It was decided that I should bring the home care assistant to meet him at the hospital so that she could explain to him what she had witnessed within the four walls of the cottage. This was a different home carer from the one who had tried to remonstrate with Pat.

During her very first visit, the second home care assistant had been so horrified by Pat's behaviour towards her grandfather that on leaving the house she had fallen into her car and driven straight to Ashton to report to her line manager, tears streaming down her face so that she could scarcely see to drive. Pat had apparently bullied her grandfather into getting out of bed, stood over him shouting while the old man tried in vain to dress himself, and refused to let Mandy, the home carer, help. After this the agonising journey down the long passage took place, Pat shouting and screaming all the while and kicking the zimmer. The boyfriend apparently stood in the living room doorway the whole time and watched silently. It was truly astonishing that Pat did all this openly in front of the home care assistant, almost as if she really believed this was the correct way to treat a frail elderly person.

To cut a regrettably long story a little shorter, a high powered case conference was held at the hospital. Pat agreed to attend the conference on condition that the district nurses and the home care assistants were barred from it! She knew that we all knew far too much about her and her family life for comfort. The meeting was chaired by a senior social worker, and it was eventually agreed that Mr T should be admitted to the cottage hospital as a long-term patient. NHS hospitals these days rarely have long-stay beds, but in this case the consultant made an exception because of the grim nature of the home conditions.

Pat was not at all happy with this decision. She was still insisting that her grandfather was actually capable of walking about and attending to his own personal care, and merely needed firm handling. Far from seeming pleased that her grandfather was being offered a free NHS bed for the rest of his life, Pat demanded that the Social Services pay for her grandfather's care at home! The senior social worker pointed out tersely that because Mr T was now so frail, his care at home would cost the department about £500 per week.

It was suspected by all concerned in this case that Pat wanted her grandfather at home partly for financial reasons. Once out of his granddaughter's clutches and safely within the confines of the hospital, Mr T's benefits would stop and Pat would no longer have access to her grandfather's pension. Turning an obdurate deaf ear to Pat's protests, the hospital staff took her grandfather in. The latter certainly voiced no objection to permanent hospital admission.

What had caused Pat to behave in this sadistic fashion towards her grandfather? Was she perhaps turning the tables on a grandfather who had been a tyrant to his children and grandchildren when they were young? Social workers who work with the elderly enter their lives towards the end when family dynamics have probably become set in a pattern for many years, and we can only speculate on what has gone before.

Mr T had been in the cottage hospital some months when the granddaughter's house was burned down to the ground in mysterious circumstances. No one was in it at the time. Was this arson? Was it a way of making money out of the insurance to compensate for the fact that Pat and her boyfriend no longer had access to her grandfather's money? These remain unanswered questions.

—o0o—

'Mr J, how about coming to sit on the sofa, near your mother, and then the three of us can have a proper talk.' Feeling decidedly inept, I continued to address an invisible person. Mr J, as usual, had seated himself on a low stool directly behind his mother's wheelchair, and was completely hidden from my view. Mrs J sat hunched and motionless in the wheelchair, her face rigid and mask-like, reminiscent of a waxwork figure in a museum, a testimony to the classic facial symptoms of

Parkinson's disease. The living room was dark and gloomy, the curtains firmly drawn and the windows tight shut, despite the heatwave. Piles of old newspapers, some of them brown with age, filled every available space on the floor, the table, the sideboard, on top of the television.

Mrs J lived with her bachelor son in a council house. He had been a teacher, but had been dismissed under a cloud and was now unemployed. What the cloud consisted of no one seemed to know, and his GP would only tell me that he had a lengthy history of mental health problems but would not elaborate. Mr J's sister, Mrs O, lived next door and worked as a legal secretary. It is said that there are people with truly Jekyll and Hyde personalities who can be one person at work and a completely different person at home. Mrs O was one of these. Held in esteem by her colleagues, she appeared to shed this persona once within the four walls of her home and assume another, darker one. Her husband was older than she and not in good health, and a distant relative expressed her concerns in a letter to the Social Services department about the way Mrs O treated her husband. He was prevented from ever leaving the house and was kept short of food.

Brother and sister were clearly part of a weird family – or, to use a politically correct expression, a dysfunctional family. My principal concern centred on the fact that Mrs J's son was the main carer, but his interpretation of 'caring' was scarcely acceptable to me. Mrs J was very frail and completely dependent on others to help her in all areas of daily living. At the behest of worried district nurses I arranged for a home care assistant to start visiting on a daily basis, but this service soon stopped because the son objected to everything the home carers tried to do for Mrs J and some of them were frankly frightened of him. Sometimes he hid for hours in a wardrobe upstairs, or he would sit downstairs, completely silent, and just stare.

One home carer tried taking Mrs J out in her wheelchair in an attempt to provide some relief from sitting helplessly in a darkened room all day without any kind of stimulation. As soon as they had gone a little way down the road towards the shopping area, Mrs J would whisper: 'Please could we go to Spar and buy a bar of chocolate. I would so love something sweet.' Cathy would oblige, and then had to push the wheelchair very slowly round the town while Mrs J furtively consumed her chocolate. The latter seemed terrified in case her son discovered that she was committing the sin of consuming sweets and chocolate. It transpired that he obsessively forced her to stick to a very rigid diet which totally excluded any 'naughty but nice' food items such as cakes or puddings, although no doctor or dietician had ever prescribed a strict diet. He did not permit her to watch TV, listen to the radio, or read. In addition to this particular form of emotional abuse, I and the occupational therapist who was also involved in the case strongly suspected the perpetration of sexual abuse. Unexplained bruising was discovered several times by the district nurse on Mrs J's inner thighs.

This unsavoury brother and sister were pillars of the parish church. Every Sunday they would wheel their mother to church to attend one of the services, a walking portrait of a God-fearing family. Underneath this pious exterior there lurked a disturbed and disturbing morass of evil motives and emotions. The parish priest, a perceptive man, took me to one side one day and asked me if the Social Services knew anything about Mrs J's home life as he felt uneasy about her offspring's attitude. I revealed to him that we did in fact know an alarming amount, and I was coming to the conclusion that Mrs J would have to be removed from her home.

This in fact is what eventually happened, although it took some time to bring about. Meanwhile Mrs O took it upon herself to harass me whenever the opportunity presented itself.

She would turn up unannounced when I arrived to meet the patch carer for a discussion, or track me down and corner me in the sheltered housing unit if I happened to be using the telephone in the warden's office. She criticised in minute detail everything Social Services personnel were trying to do for her mother, and in the end refused to allow the home carers to have access to the house. I felt sure she was colluding with her brother.

Mrs J grew ever more frail, and the GP who was the only individual now permitted to visit Mrs J, and that only occasionally, eventually conceded that 'something will have to be done'. That something, with Mrs J's consent, was admission to a nursing home in Eastbury. By this time the case had passed out of my hands, but Mrs O and her brother continued to haunt the department, Mrs O in the form of a storm of critical, scathing letters, and Mr J through the medium of telephone calls, mainly to the occupational therapist, which sometimes consisted of nothing more substantial than heavy breathing.

Dealing with difficult relatives is inevitably part and parcel of a social worker's everyday work. Not all relatives are difficult, by any means, as I have already stated. Some are devoted to their parents, auntie, disabled brother, whoever it happens to be, and form very good relationships with the social worker who is trying to help and alleviate an often distressing situation. Others, however, turn out to be the bane to end all banes, and the social worker wonders wearily what on earth she can have done in a former life to merit such an ordeal by fire. A difficult person compounds the situation still further if he or she is suspected of abuse.

In some ways, the most difficult case I have dealt with in recent years was 83-year-old Bessie, who was admitted to the assessment unit at Winfield from her home in a nearby village following an acute episode of mental confusion, which led her allegedly to make sexual advances to several inhabitants in the vicinity. If Bessie had been the sole individual in the case, the situation would have been quite straightforward and relatively simple. However, Bessie had a nephew.

Before her admission to hospital Bessie was not known to any agency. She had lived on her own since her husband's death ten years previously and had managed well with the minimum of support from a private cleaning lady and one or two neighbours. She was still driving and doing her own shopping and had a gentleman friend in Honeystone whom she saw regularly.

During her spell in the assessment unit it was ascertained that Bessie's bout of confused behaviour had been largely caused by a particular heart problem plus, probably, a series of small strokes. She soon became lucid again, apart from intermittent bouts of mild confusion, and was able to attend to all her personal care needs. The staff needed to do little for her. Consequently at the case conference held to thrash out plans for Bessie's future, all present agreed that Bessie could return home and was not eligible for our home care.

All, that is, except Bessie's nephew, Mr X. Bessie very much wanted to live in her own home and to be as independent as possible, but Mr X maintained that she needed 24-hour care, and only reluctantly agreed to my suggestion that a move into sheltered housing a few miles from her old home would be ideal for her. The village where she had lived for many years had no shop or other amenities, and the doctor told her she must relinquish her driving licence.

Once Bessie was installed in a small flat within a warden-controlled sheltered housing unit, the fun and games really started. Mr X refused to accept our assessment of his aunt's capabilities and continued to insist to all and sundry that she should be in residential care. He employed a home carer from a private agency who very quickly found out that she was largely superfluous. Mr X had instructed her to spend several hours every day getting his aunt up, washed, dressed, and breakfasted, and then to provide other meals for her and carry out sundry practical tasks such as bed-making and shopping.

At first the home care assistant felt bewildered, then her bewilderment turned to anger. It became clear to her that Bessie was perfectly capable of washing, boiling her breakfast egg, etc and did not need her or anyone to do these things for her, and indeed wanted to be independent. Mr X had bombarded her with minute instructions which included exactly what his aunt was to eat and not eat. She had absolutely no choice in this matter or in any other facet of her life. She was not even permitted to open her own mail. The day she moved into the new flat Mr X told other tenants in the building that his aunt was 'severely confused', despite the fact that the community psychiatric nurse (CPN) maintained that in her professional opinion, she was but mildly muddled.

I arrived back from a fortnight's leave to find a positive snowstorm of messages waiting for me, most of which concerned Bessie. By that time she had been in her new flat for about three weeks. The home carer and the warden were ready to explode as a result of verbal sparring matches, mostly conducted on the telephone, with Mr X.

Mr X's insistence that his aunt should eat ham sandwiches and nothing but ham sandwiches every day for her lunch proved to be the straw that broke the camel's back. After about a week of this monotonous fare, Bessie asked the home carer if she could possibly have a change of menu. She asked her to make suggestions, and went out and bought her some cheese.

Later that day she received yet another telephone call from Mr X, who had taken to telephoning certain people involved in the case on numerous occasions, sometimes several times a day. The home care assistant, goaded beyond endurance, told

Mr X that his aunt was able and indeed wanted to do most things for herself, which included deciding what to eat. Mr X immediately accused her of taking her aunt's money, told her she was fired, and reported her to the police. The police refused to take the matter further on the grounds that not a shred of evidence existed.

After perusing these messages and speaking to both the warden and the home carer, I wearily decided that I would have to remonstrate with Mr X, who had already decided to lodge a formal complaint against the Social Services department because we did not agree that Bessie needed 24-hour care or met our departmental criteria for the provision of home care.

This difficult nephew was what I would describe as a 'serial complainer'. He had clearly absorbed like a sponge all the negative criticism of social workers and their departments discernible like a disapproving refrain in all branches of the media, and become totally convinced that every Social Services department was rotten and decadent. He was the type of person who revelled in complaining about everything from broken-down trains to prurient window cleaners.

In a letter I suggested to Mr X that another, much less formal meeting be held at a venue of his choice, to discuss his aunt's care needs as he had been so critical of the way the case conference had been conducted. However, he flatly refused to concede to this suggestion and also to two other suggestions, made during the succeeding months by other people, to meetings or get-togethers. This stalemate continued for six months with Mr X and his equally formidable sister barging their way unsuccessfully through each stage of our formal complaints procedure.

Bessie herself was a pleasant, sometimes slightly confused woman, who was basically lonely and depressed because of the trauma of the lengthy spell in hospital, losing her previous home in the village she loved, and no longer being permitted to drive. The frail elderly suffer many losses such as bereavement, loss of mobility, loss of sight or hearing; but one blow that almost invariably receives scant attention is having to stop driving. A person who has driven a car throughout his or her adult life finds the sudden loss of independence very hard to adjust to, and generally regards it as another depressing step on the road to total helplessness and dependence. Bessie seemed somewhat embarrassed by her nephew's attitude and antics and tried to laugh them off by saying to me and others: 'He's an old fuss-pot, you know' or 'He's a rather over-anxious person, just like his mother used to be', although she never criticised him in a negative fashion.

Signs of unwelcome sexual activity never reappeared, and her very good GP, with whom I liaised regularly throughout the six months, was privately of the opinion that Bessie had never constituted a sexual nuisance to anyone. However, the story of her 'mental instability' was circulated by her nephew amongst the other tenants, who looked askance at her as if she were likely to jump out at them from a dark corner at any moment. This did not help her feelings of loneliness. I attempted to alleviate this sense of isolation by arranging for a voluntary visitor to befriend her, call upon her at home for a chat and take her out for a walk or to the shops, which she greatly appreciated. However, this had to be done by stealth behind her nephew's back as he would soon have scuppered any arrangement made by me.

Mr X did not live locally, but many miles away in Eastern Scotland. This did not prevent him from calling himself his aunt's carer, a complete misnomer in view of the fact that he visited her about every five or six weeks, and then only spent an hour or two with her. He made enormous efforts to clamp down on every area of her daily life by remote control. He hired another private home care assistant, taking care this time to choose a young woman with a timid manner and no experience of working with the elderly, who was completely incapable of standing up to Mr X.

I became increasingly concerned about Bessie's enforced lifestyle, imposed upon her by a control freak in the shape of her nephew whose behaviour must surely have indicated some kind of mental illness. As stated before, abuse of an adult can take many forms. In this case the abuse was overwhelmingly psychological, emotional, and financial. The client was deprived of choice. She was not permitted to handle money, read her own letters, choose what to eat, or carry out normal daily activities within her own flat. It clearly never occurred to her nephew to consult his aunt about the desirability of employing a home care assistant, or to invite her to take part in the interviewing and selection process. She was looked upon as a mindless imbecile.

It became crystal clear early on in this process that establishing any kind of positive relationship with Mr X was out of the question. Anyone who disagreed with his methods of dealing with his aunt was immediately labelled as an enemy, while those who did not oppose him were awarded several Brownie points. He spent an astonishing amount of time compiling lengthy letters and making countless telephone calls to lodge complaints against me and my senior in particular, as well as several other individuals. He was determined to achieve his objective of having his aunt admitted to residential care, and this he did by what I can only describe as bulldozing and steamrollering.

He would wear down certain key individuals until they could stand no more. At frequent intervals he demanded a re-assessment of his aunt's situation and clearly wanted a change of social worker. This my team manager, who was most supportive throughout this nightmarish period, firmly refused to accede to, and on one occasion he even accompanied me on an assessment visit to Bessie so that he could see for himself what all the fuss was about. His view of the situation was the same as mine: Bessie was clearly capable of managing her daily life with the minimum of support, despite various physical ailments and bouts of confusion. The young timid home carer was calling once per day to provide Bessie with a main meal; everything else she did for herself, a lifestyle which frankly belied her nephew's portrayal of him as a helpless victim who was too confused to articulate her needs or look after herself.

Mr X then decided to concentrate on the hapless GP whom he considered to be a key pawn in his scheme. He bombarded the surgery with telephone calls until the receptionists began to rebel. Off the cuff the GP told me that Bessie's file had attained the distinction of being the fattest patient file in the surgery due mainly to all the telephone calls, carefully recorded, and a number of letters. Mr X tried to convince the doctor that Bessie was suffering from the consequences of neglect because the Social Services refused to provide care at home or residential care.

Latterly Bessie had been suffering from what seemed to be panic attacks at night, convinced she was suffering from serious illness and perhaps about to die. She started making frequent nocturnal telephone calls to the surgery and obliging the warden, despite the fact that she was off-duty at night, to come to her flat to calm things down. This anxiety state was probably induced by her nephew's determination to brainwash her into believing that she was at great risk and in need of 24-hour supervision.

Eventually Mr X managed to push the GP into having Bessie admitted to a local home on a temporary basis. He and his sister were jubilant and travelled to -----shire to attend a conference at which they succeeded, by means of a type of blackmail, in turning all present into sycophantic zombies who sat meekly and muttered 'Yes, Mr X', 'Oh no, Miss X', while the pair railed against the department's handling of the case. I was not present as I had requested a change of social worker shortly after Bessie's admission to residential care. There are limits to every social worker's powers of endurance.

If anyone at the conference so much as dared to show the slightest sign of disagreeing with Mr and Miss X, they immediately threatened to 'go to the papers' or 'give the 10 o'clock News a juicy bit of scandal to announce'. That afternoon the air was alive with the hum of faxes flying to and from various senior managers, who likewise were bulldozed into agreeing to Mr X's demand that his aunt be given a permanent residential place.

The upshot of this appalling chain of events was that the case was referred to the Ombudsman who, in the fullness of time, published her decision that she did not uphold Mr X's complaint. And all this came about because I and others were determined to hang on to the important social work principle of treating a client as an individual who is capable of making choices.

Chapter Seveteen

April 2001. Foot and mouth had struck many counties, and the ripple effect had permeated virtually all strata of life. Only those who actually lived through this surreal, bizarre and gruesome experience in one of the affected areas can ever really appreciate its truly traumatic effect. Almost overnight, parts of rural Britain which had never before featured in the media became the focus of every national and international newspaper and TV channel. Hitherto unheard of villages suddenly became cluttered with journalists from every quarter of the globe. On the front of French, German, Dutch and American newspapers displayed outside a newsagent in Eastbury, I caught sight of articles on and pictures of -----shire villages, farmland and livestock, telling the awful story in sensational mode.

The heaps of rotting carcases, the gigantic fires which burnt for weeks and which could be seen, like sinister beacons, for many miles around, the all-pervading stench, the weeping farmers, the barred-off roads and footpaths, the gallons of disinfectant – all this has been chronicled and portrayed ad infinitum, so I will not add to it.

A being who had just arrived from another planet and knew nothing of the foot and mouth crisis might have been forgiven for thinking that a military coup had come about in -----shire: after the army had arrived with orders to sort out the chaos, all the roads in and around Eastbury were thick with army trucks and Land Rovers. The sight of soldiers everywhere became commonplace. One Monday morning I spotted a weary looking soldier sitting in the driving seat of his Land Rover in the car park of our local Tesco, assiduously shaving himself, presumably after an all-night stint at the nearby burial ground.

Because of my strong views on animal welfare and feelings of extreme distaste for certain unacceptable farming practices, I had mixed feelings about the predicament of farmers and the much publicised 'plight' of the many thousands of slaughtered farm animals. Many of those same animals would have met with a much more barbaric fate in so-called 'normal' times, as part of the unspeakable live export trade.

As a social worker I was enmeshed willy nilly with the full horror of the situation. To my profound dismay, however, my movements were greatly restricted. I did not go to Ashton for many weeks, or to the remote rural area beyond Ashton for many months, for fear of spreading the disease. Some of my clients, those who did not belong to the farming community, were puzzled and distressed by my prolonged absence. Home care assistants, relatives and others did their best to explain why I was obliged to confine myself largely to the office in Eastbury and organise as much as possible by telephone and letter.

The smog-ridden hell which the citizens of Ashton were forced to endure, while dozens of funeral pyres were spewing forth toxic fumes from the scores of farms surrounding the town, was a scandal which should never have happened. In Ashton and elsewhere in -----shire, the plight of those running small businesses ruined or nearly ruined by a crisis which was not of their making has been neither sufficiently highlighted nor compensated. I and others who work in related fields, such as the local GPs and district nurses, have had to listen to some sorry tales which never found their way into the newspapers. After all, of what importance in the eyes of the media is, for example, a small hairdressing business or a small sports shop that has gone to the wall in a little unimportant town? Such sorrowful experiences are not glamorous or sensational enough to sell papers or burst upon TV screens.

The preceding year, the dawn of a new century, had been one of unwelcome notoriety for Winfield, our local psychiatric hospital. A scandal regarding two long-stay wards for the elderly was uncovered and an uncomfortably large number of medical staff named and shamed, both locally and nationally. To say that we social workers were dismayed by the revelations is an understatement. Abuse, rough handling and ridicule of frail dementia sufferers had clearly taken place, but I personally had not felt concerned when clients of mine were admitted to one or other of these wards. One, a colourful nonagenarian named Dolly, who had survived four husbands and several boyfriends, and who still, at the time of admission, had a boyfriend in tow, had to be sectioned under the Mental Health Act.

Dolly settled down well on the ward and eventually came to look upon it as her home before eventually moving into residential care. Her boyfriend Hamish, a mere slip of a 70-year-old, was just as colourfully eccentric and took to calling at the ward at unusual hours, such as 3am, sometimes under the influence. The ward staff coped with this situation with vigour and tact, in my view. Hamish was not discouraged from visiting Dolly, but he was firmly educated into calling at more appropriate times. During visiting hours they were frequently to be seen sitting one on each side of the open fire in the day room, like a cosy married couple.

The old Winfield hospital has now gone, the sprawling complex of ageing buildings deserted and silent. Meadow

View Clinic is the new establishment, a fresh name heralding a fresh start in 2001, concentrating mainly on short-term care and day care for people with a wide variety of mental health problems.

For over 20 years as a social worker, I had regular contact with various wards within Winfield, and I felt strongly that an erroneous picture of the hospital was inevitably portrayed by the media. Only the negative and rotten aspects of two wards hit the headlines. None of the good work undertaken every day in other wards by a whole variety of staff was ever brought to the attention of the public.

This infuriating and destructive tendency on the part of the media always to focus on the negative and ignore the positive aspects of an organisation has blighted the social work profession for at least 20 years. Only those Social Services staff who gritted their teeth through 18 years of Conservative government, during which social care staff became completely demoralised by the continual belittling of their work and their profession, can have any clear understanding of how discouraging this was. The government stance was adopted eagerly by the more right-wing press, until the general public gradually became brainwashed into believing that all social workers were, at best, ill-educated nincompoops and, at worst, vicarious child killers. But where were all these idle, incompetent, disorganised social workers and feckless team managers? I would wonder to myself in bewilderment. Of the social work staff with whom I had worked or liaised throughout the whole of my lengthy career, fewer than the fingers on one hand could actually be described as useless pieces of dead wood. If asked at any kind of social gathering what work I did, I eventually ceased to say 'social worker' because these two words frequently provoked an eloquent look or comment of disapproval or even disgust on the part of the questioner. I learnt merely to say vaguely, 'Oh, I work for the local authority', then adroitly change the subject as soon as possible.

I knew that the year 2001 would be the last year of my working life. Looking round me at my colleagues in our open plan office, what did I see? Weary, cynical social workers battling with constant change (the kaleidoscope was being shaken continually now, and the ever-changing patterns never allowed to linger) and steadily increasing caseloads, and I reflected that New Labour's attitude towards the social work profession was a little more positive and encouraging, but still left much to be desired.

Certain senior politicians, who ought to know better, still display a deeply worrying ignorance of how social work teams are constructed and organised today. The notion that generic teams are still widespread, and that this genericism is responsible for terrible tragedies because social workers are not specialising in one particular client group, and thereby not acquiring in-depth skills but dabbling in a dilettante fashion with all client groups, is erroneous and hopelessly out of date. Throughout Britain the vast majority of social work departments have each consisted of a number of specialist teams for at least the past 12 years. Just a glance at situations vacant pages of a journal such as 'Community Care' will confirm this. Virtually all the jobs advertised are situated within specialist teams.

Neither is it correct to maintain that a large number of social workers are frighteningly young. Where are all these green, Lolita-like social care staff? The truth of the matter is that times have changed and few social workers under the age of 30 enter the profession nowadays. Many are older, having acquired experience in another sphere. It seems the media, and many in government, will never change their spots. From time to time terrible things happen, such as the death of a child, usually at the hands of a family member. If a social worker is involved in the case, that worker is invariably cast by the media in the role of ogre. But this is not the true story of social work.

December 2001. Time to bow out. As I left the office and walked down the steps to the front entrance on the very last day for the very last time, weighed down with flowers, cards and messages from kind colleagues, clients, and their families, a thought suddenly struck me. It was all of 37 years since that far-off afternoon in 1964 when, as a timid 22-year-old, I had first arrived in Sheffield to take that faltering step into the unknown: a career in social work.

Epilogue

My car sped on as fast as I dared push it, along the meandering country lane. Patches of dappled shade alternated with stretches of almost blinding sunshine. Through gaps in the rustling beech hedges and gently soughing branches could be glimpsed intermittently the glorious landscape like a giant rolled out carpet designed with a pattern of green squares and oblongs interspersed with clumps of huge and ancient trees. Scarcely a single human habitation to be seen. The occasional church tower half hidden amongst a protective curtain of green foliage. One of the few remaining unsullied corners of rural England.

A sharp bend in the road loomed ahead. I must slow down, I reflected. Despite the scarcity of traffic, one never knew what vehicle might be lurking, concealed from view, round the bend, and there were too many horrifying accidents on country roads. As I was not familiar with this particular lane, I must take extra care.

But what was this? This vision, this dream-like image of a large house, a mansion in ruins, no roof, a shell with crumbling walls and glassless windows, set amongst the lush expanse of parkland. All thought of careful driving flew from my head as my car swerved onto the wrong side of the road, just round the bend. It surely must be Thornfield Hall after the fire, as Jane Eyre had seen it, coming suddenly upon it in her search for Mr Rochester following her long absence.

Slowing right down to a crawl, I managed to steer the car back onto the right side of the road. I was not asleep, this was not a dream, and there was no time to stop and explore. I had to drive on to keep my appointment with a new client, yet another elderly person in need of our services. As soon as I could spare the time I would find someone local who could tell me the story behind the phantom-like ruin.

So on I drove, still entranced by what I had seen, and feeling once again almost overawed by the realisation that to work in such a magical rural environment, rich in surprises, was a privilege. Past an isolated church, through a hamlet and on again into wilder country. Up a narrow track, and then I must turn left into a still narrower track, the doctor had said when giving me directions on the telephone.

The young, doubtless still idealistic medic had expressed great concern about this nonagenarian who lived in a cottage several miles from her nearest neighbour without water, electricity, gas or sanitation. She drew water from a well in the garden and made use of a chamber pot. Her GP could scarcely believe that such conditions still existed. The Hannah Hauxwells of this world are clearly not confined to Yorkshire, I reflected as I bumped to a halt in front of a low, whitewashed dwelling.

The door opened as I walked up the neat front path. A very elderly lady, white hair in a bun on top of her head, waited on the threshold.

'Please come in. You must be the lady from the welfare. Dr Maxwell told me you would call,' said this dignified 95-year-old.

Yes, I am not the social worker or the care manager, or any other fashionable appellation of the late twentieth century. I am the lady from the welfare.